Welcome to the magical world of colors! This enchanting coloring book is specifically designed for children aged 3 to 11, inviting them to embark on a vibrant journey of creativity and imagination. Within these pages, young artists will discover a captivating array of whimsical illustrations, waiting to be brought to life with the stroke of a crayon or the splash of a paintbrush.
So, grab your favorite colors, embark on this colorful adventure, and let the magic of creativity unfold on each and every page. Happy coloring!

Ricardo Silveira
2024

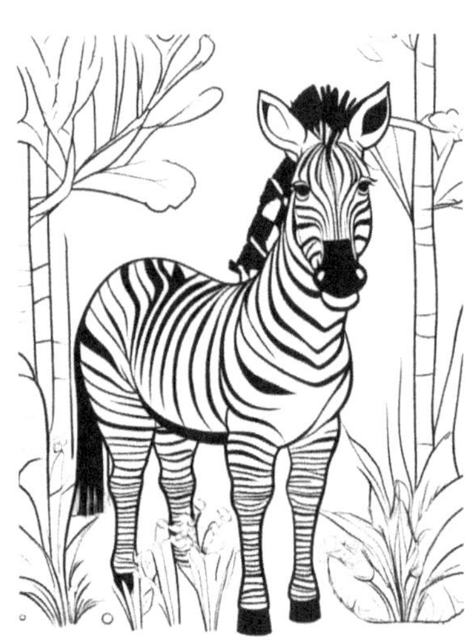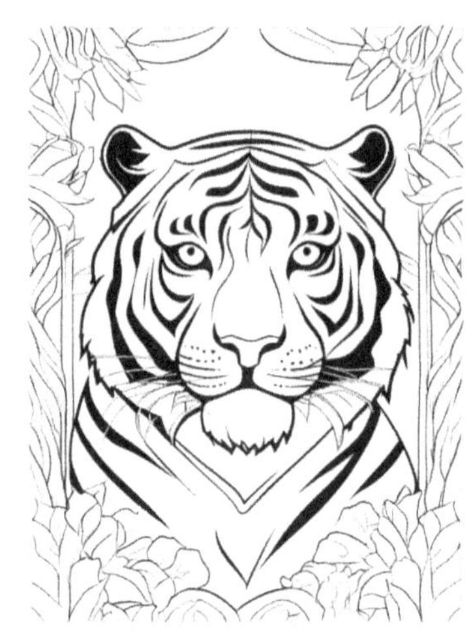

This Book Belongs to:

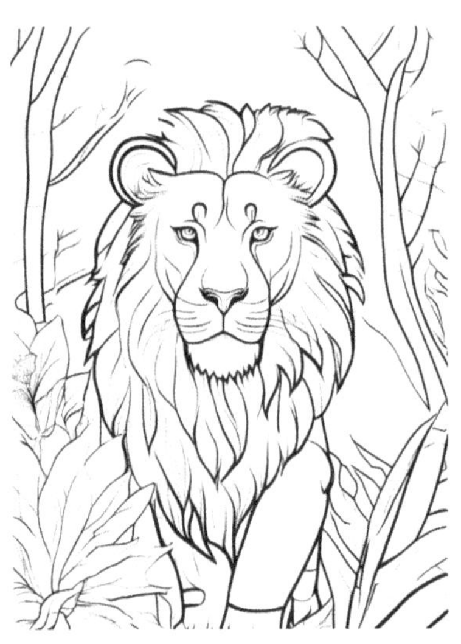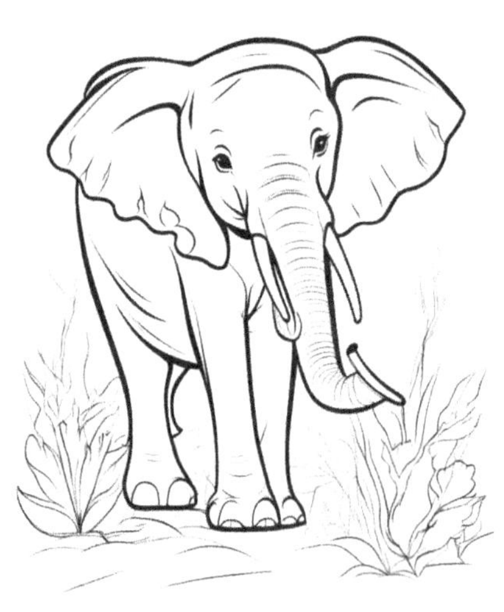

Test Color Page

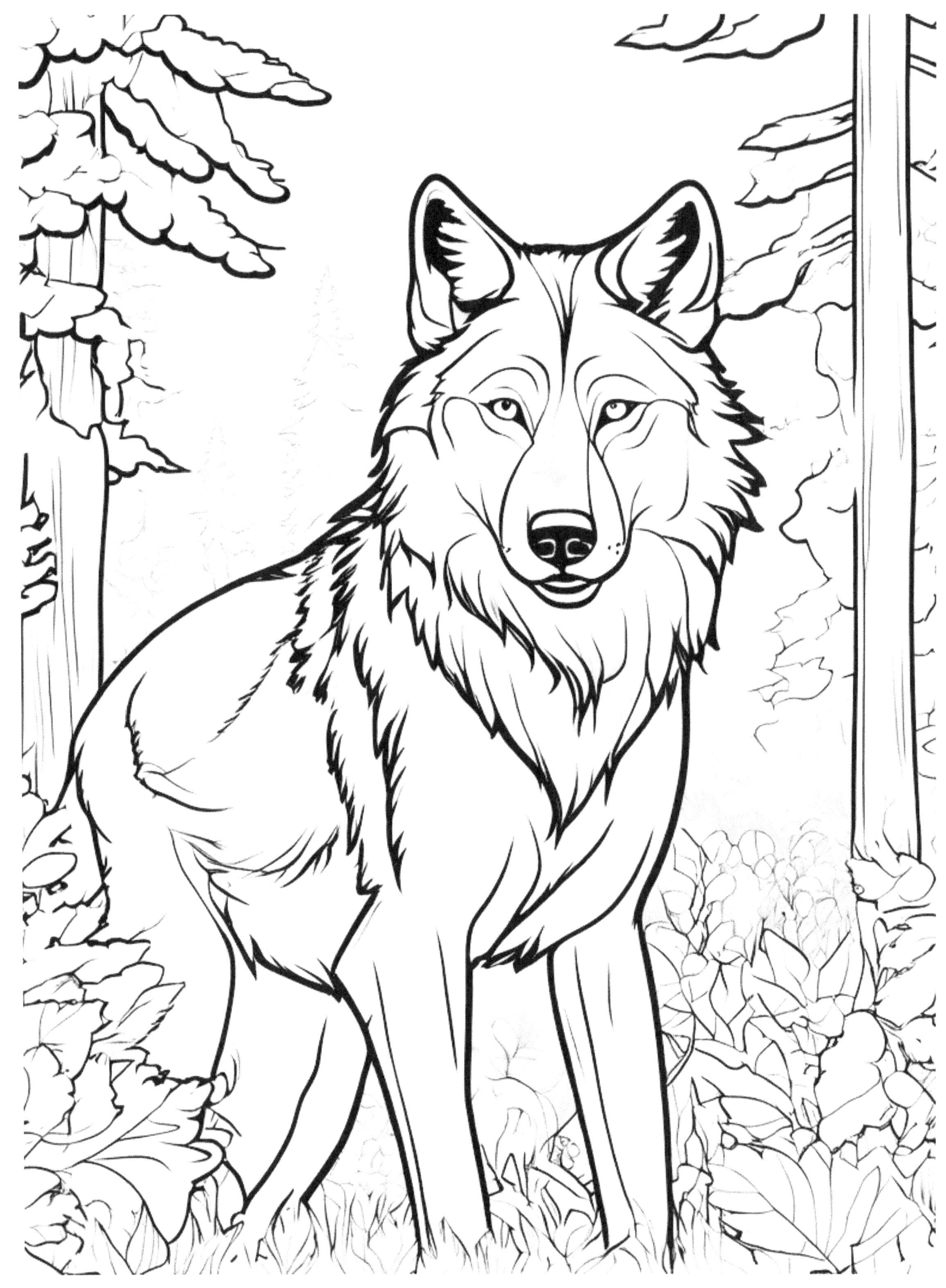

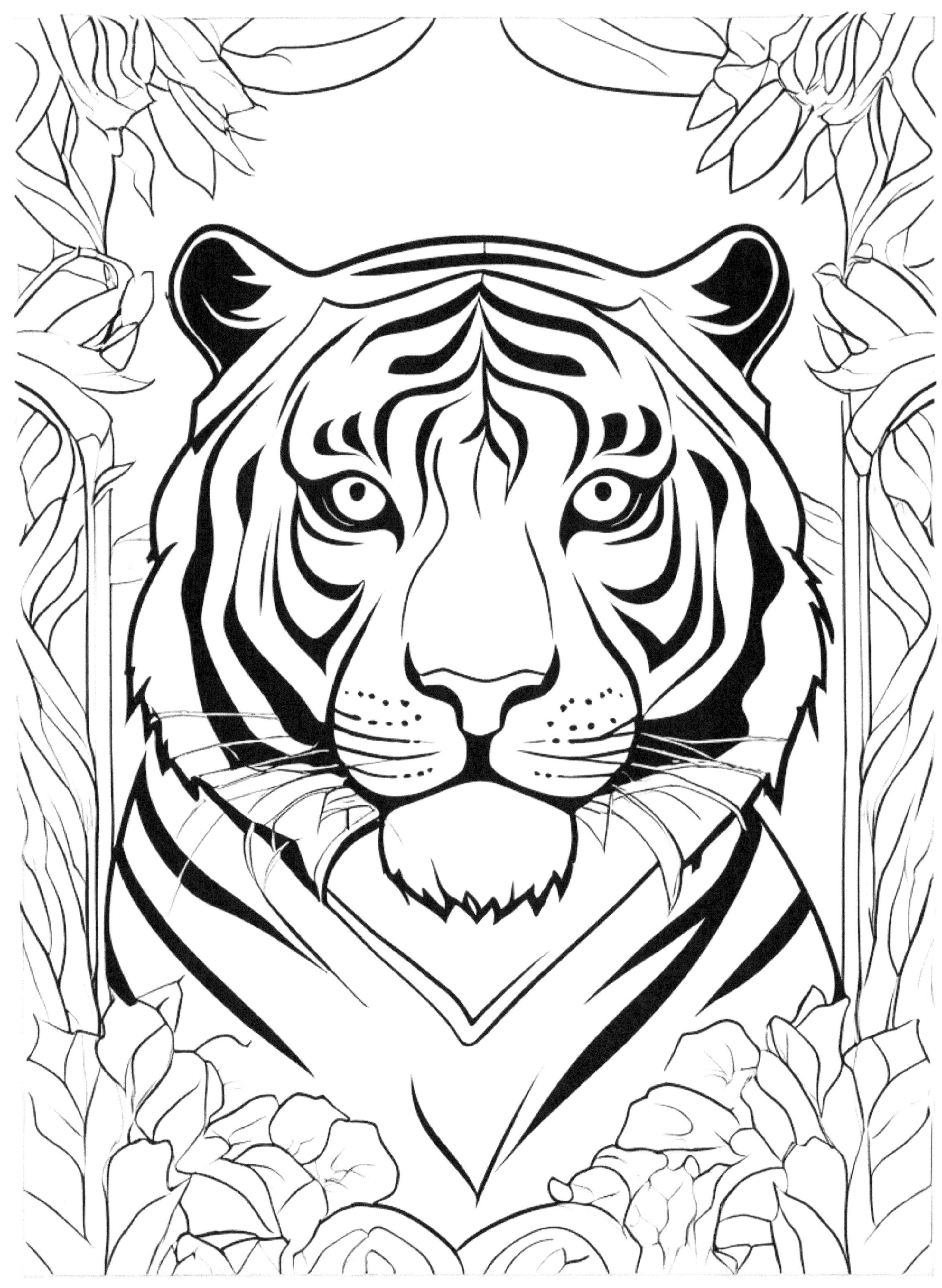

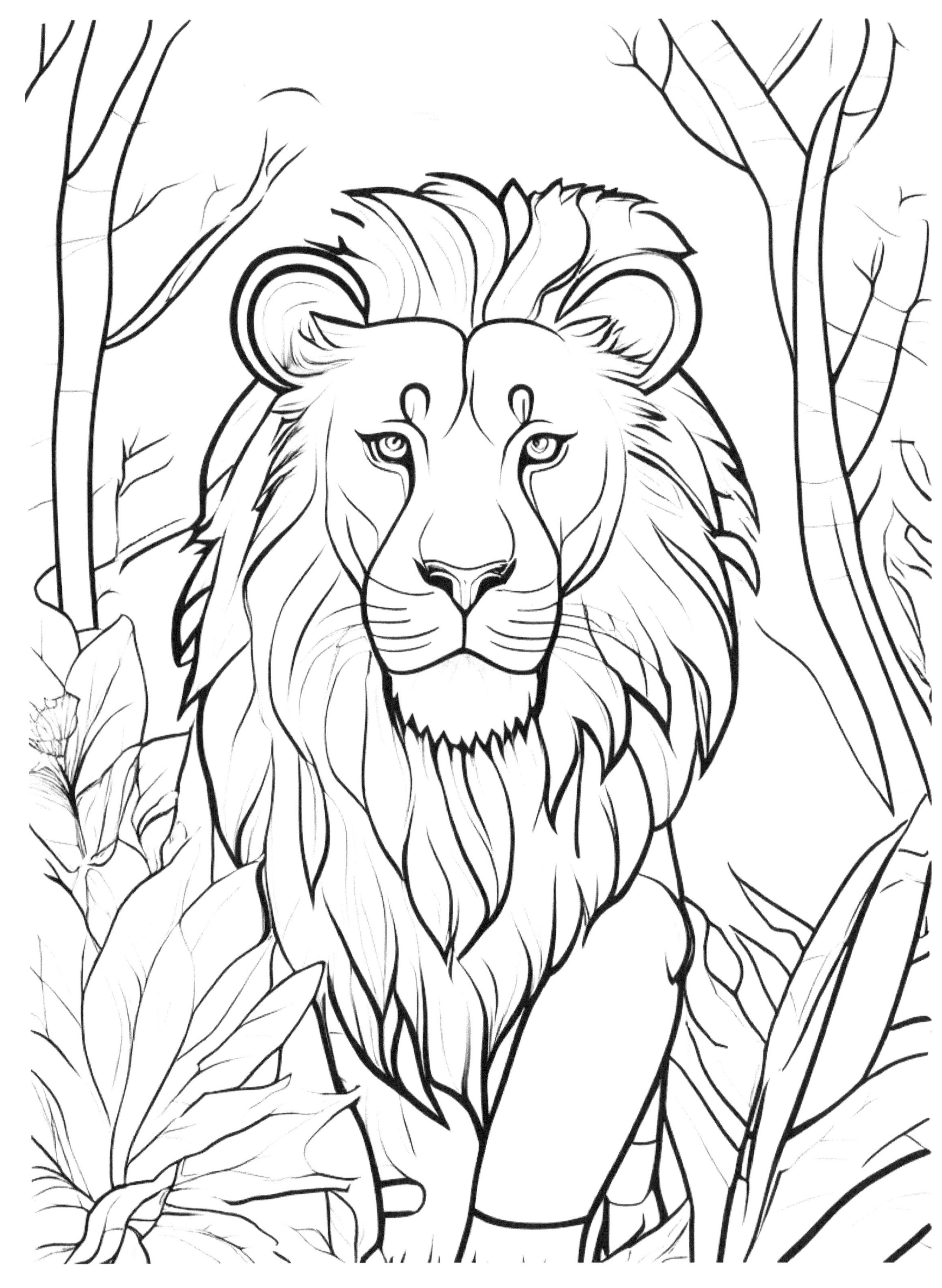

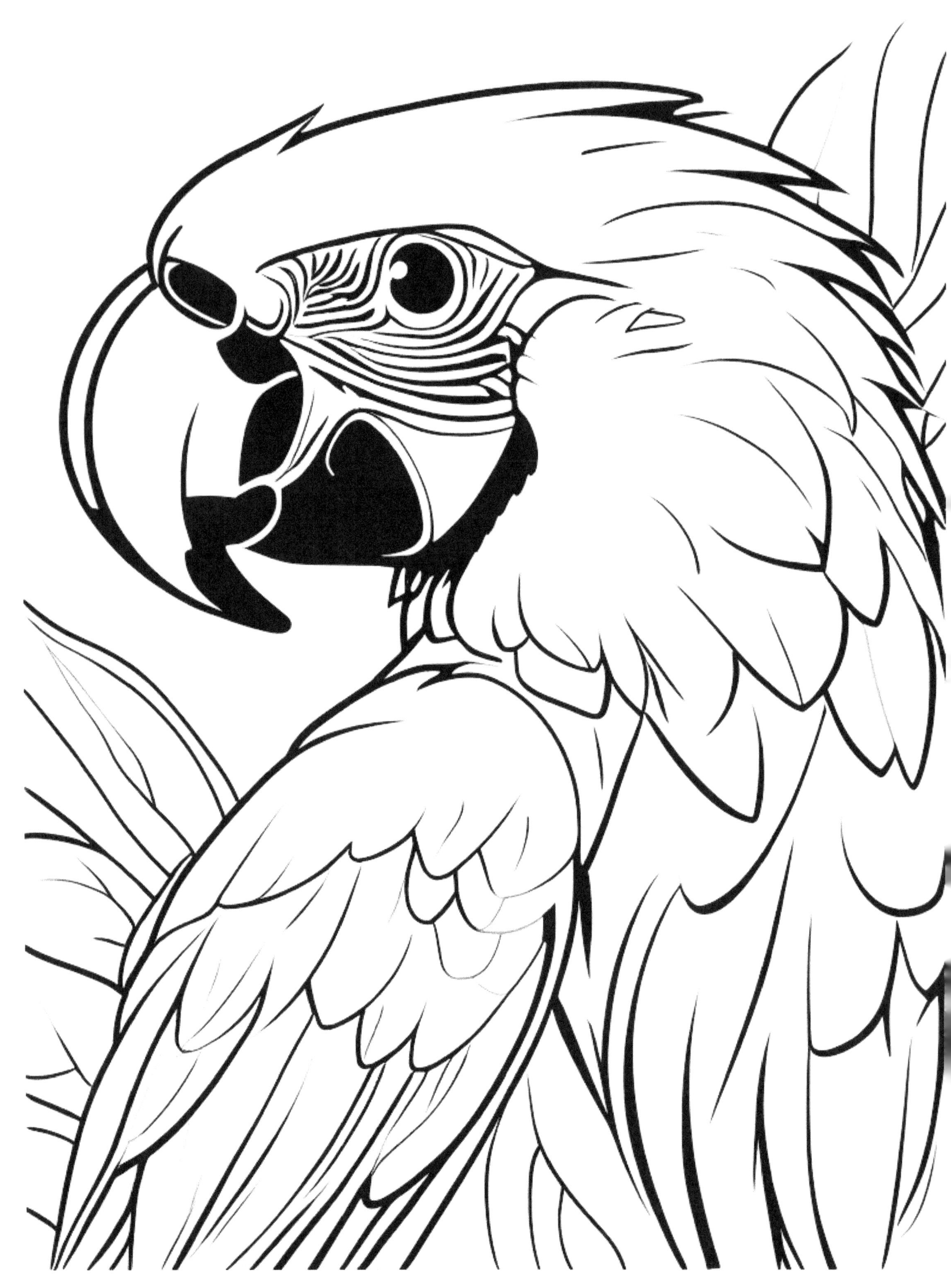

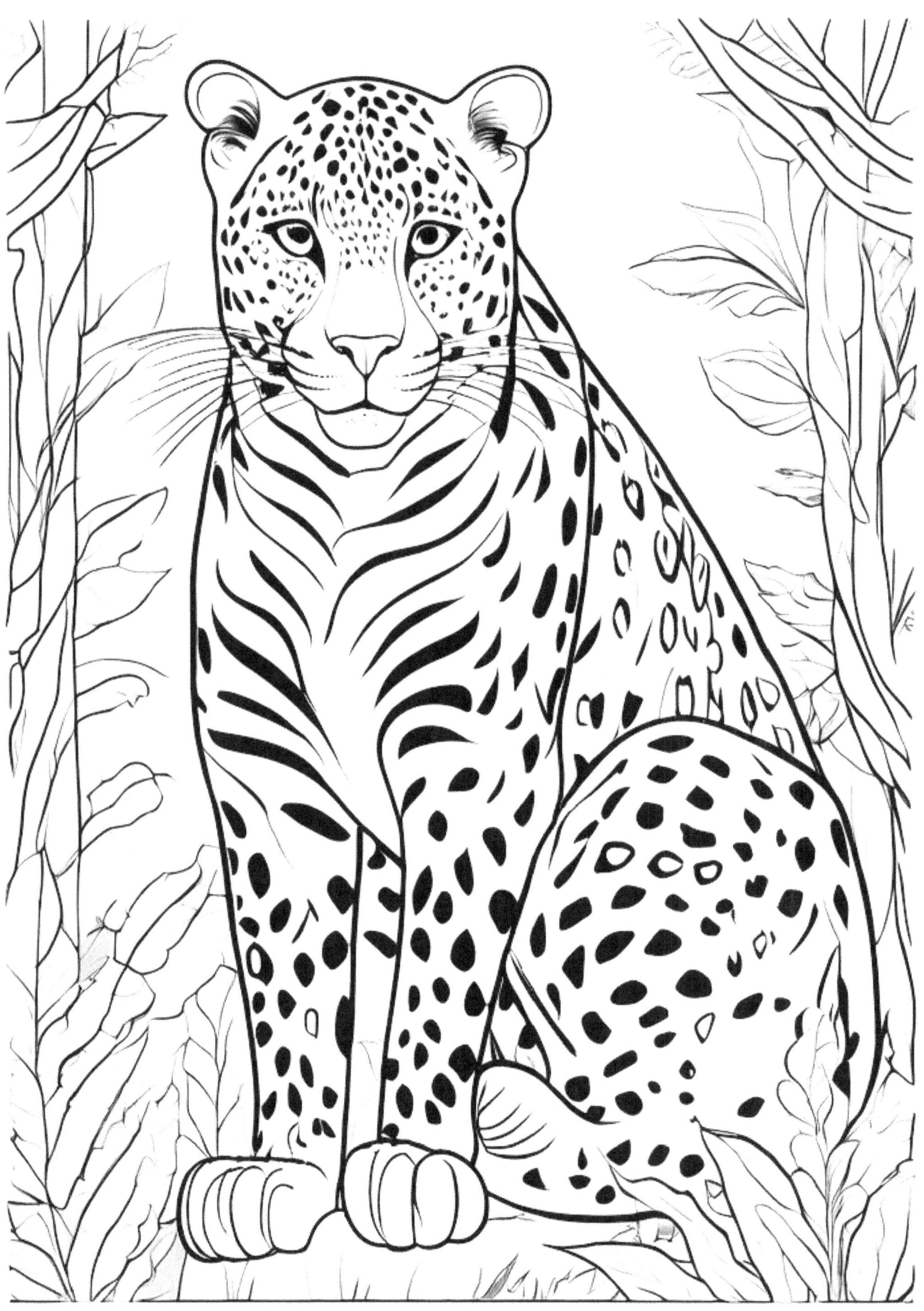

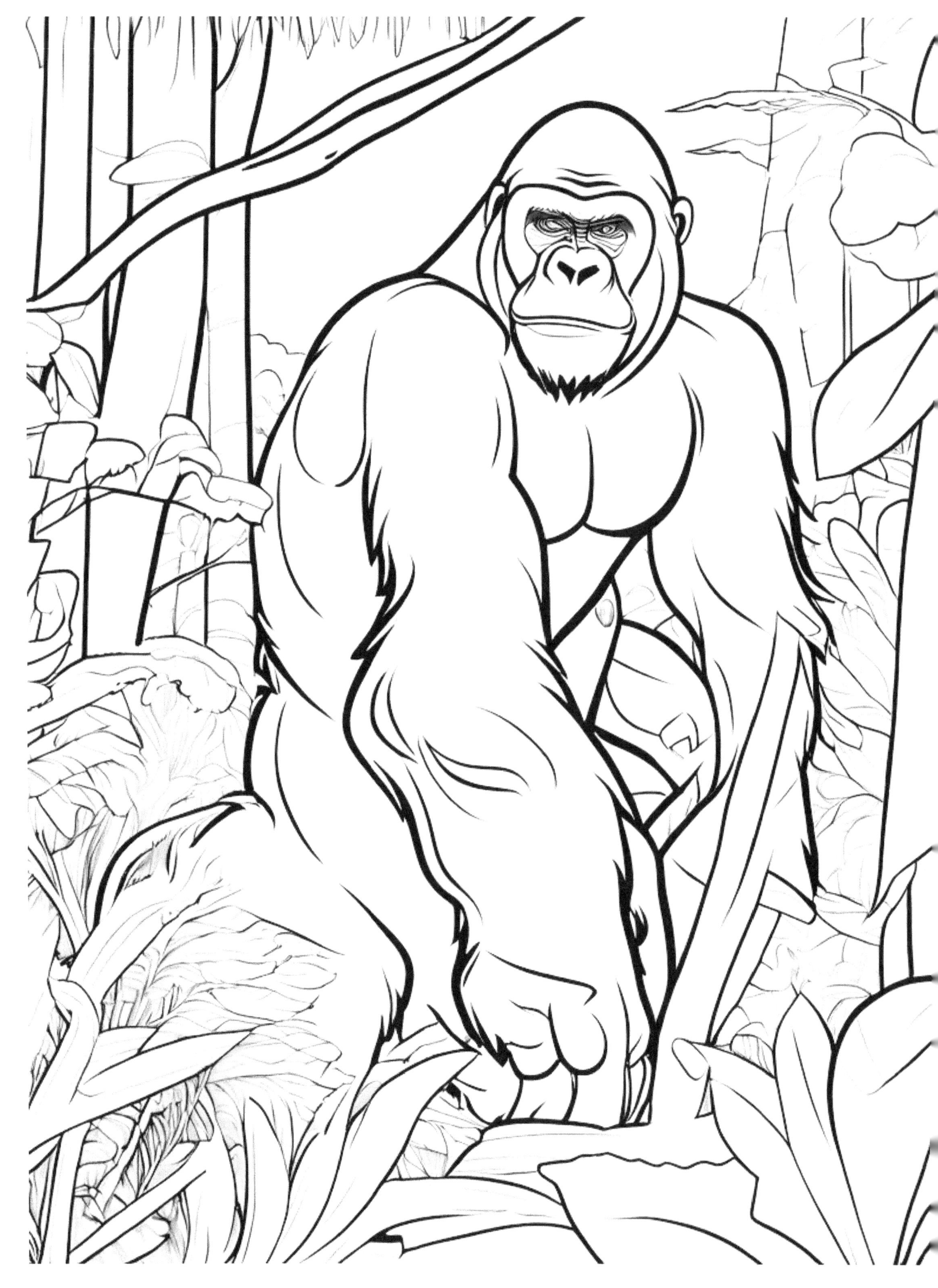

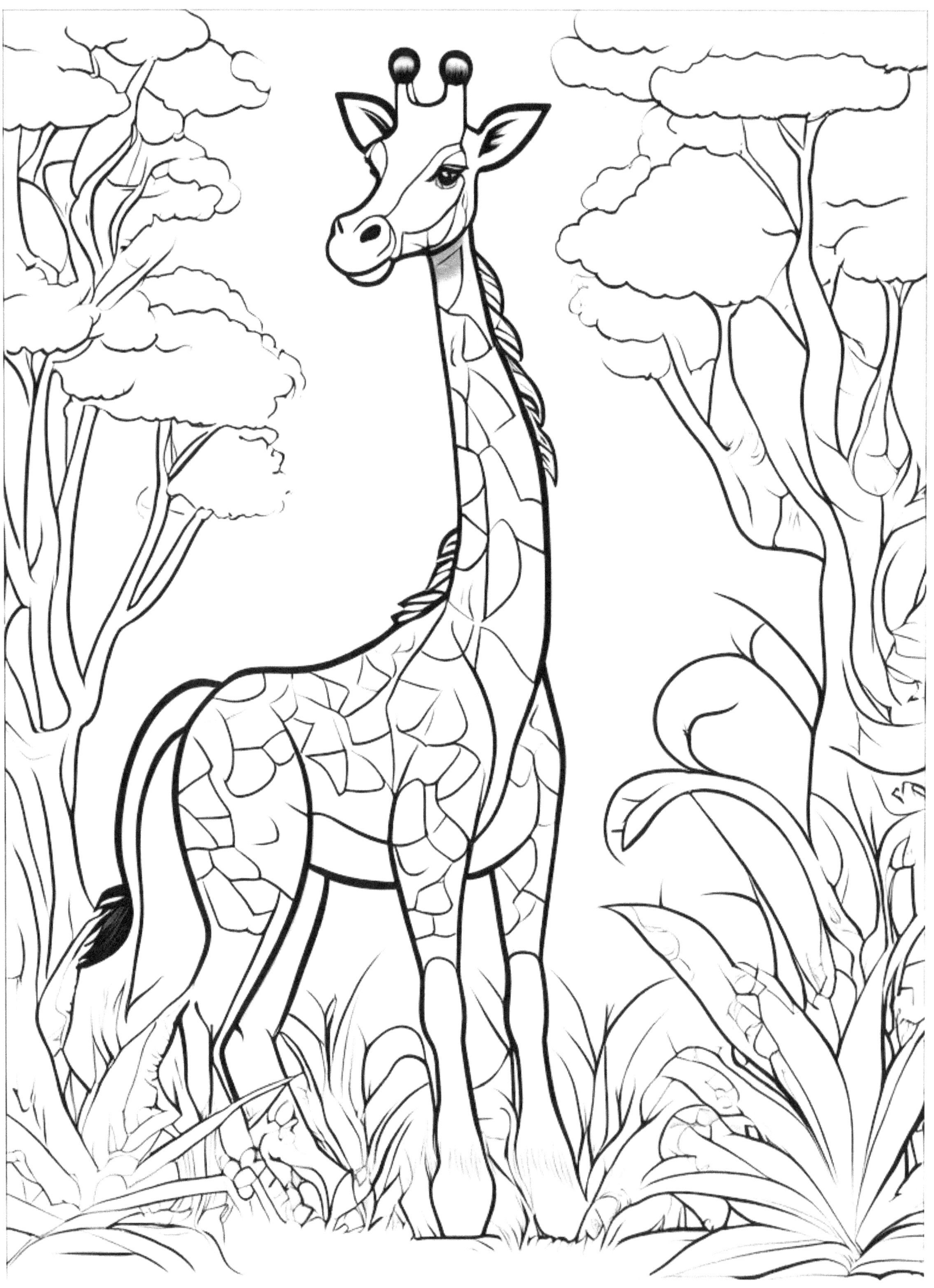

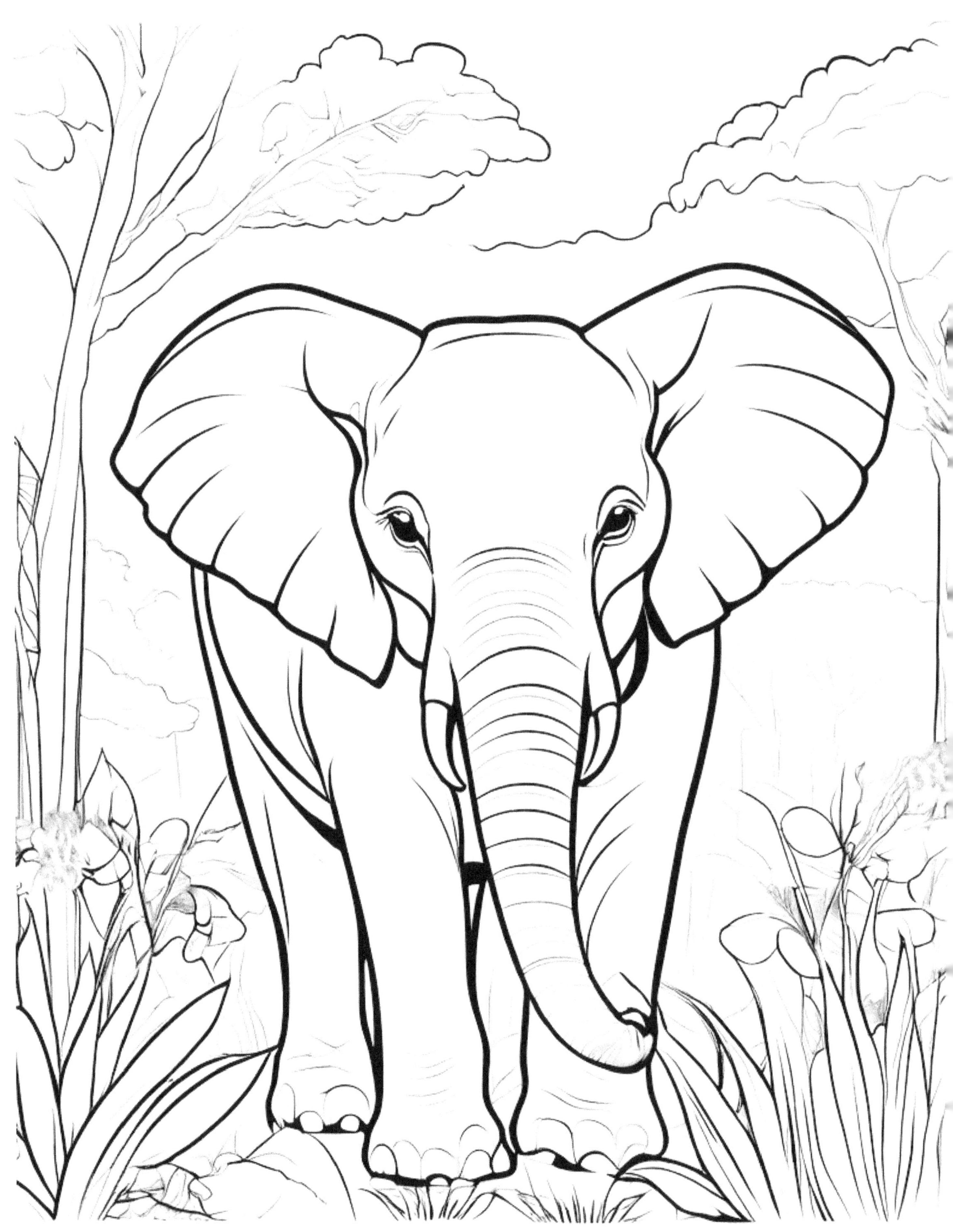

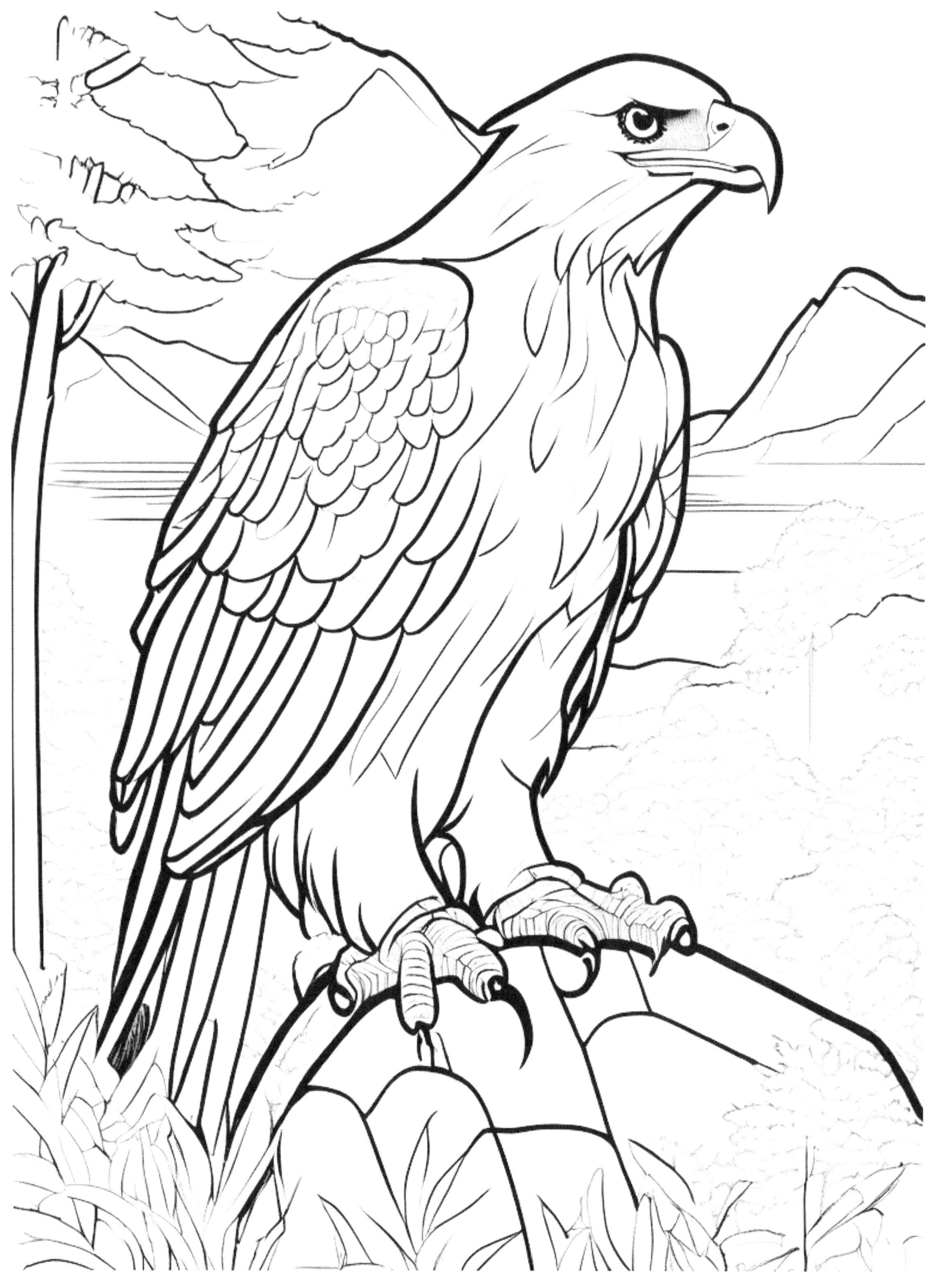

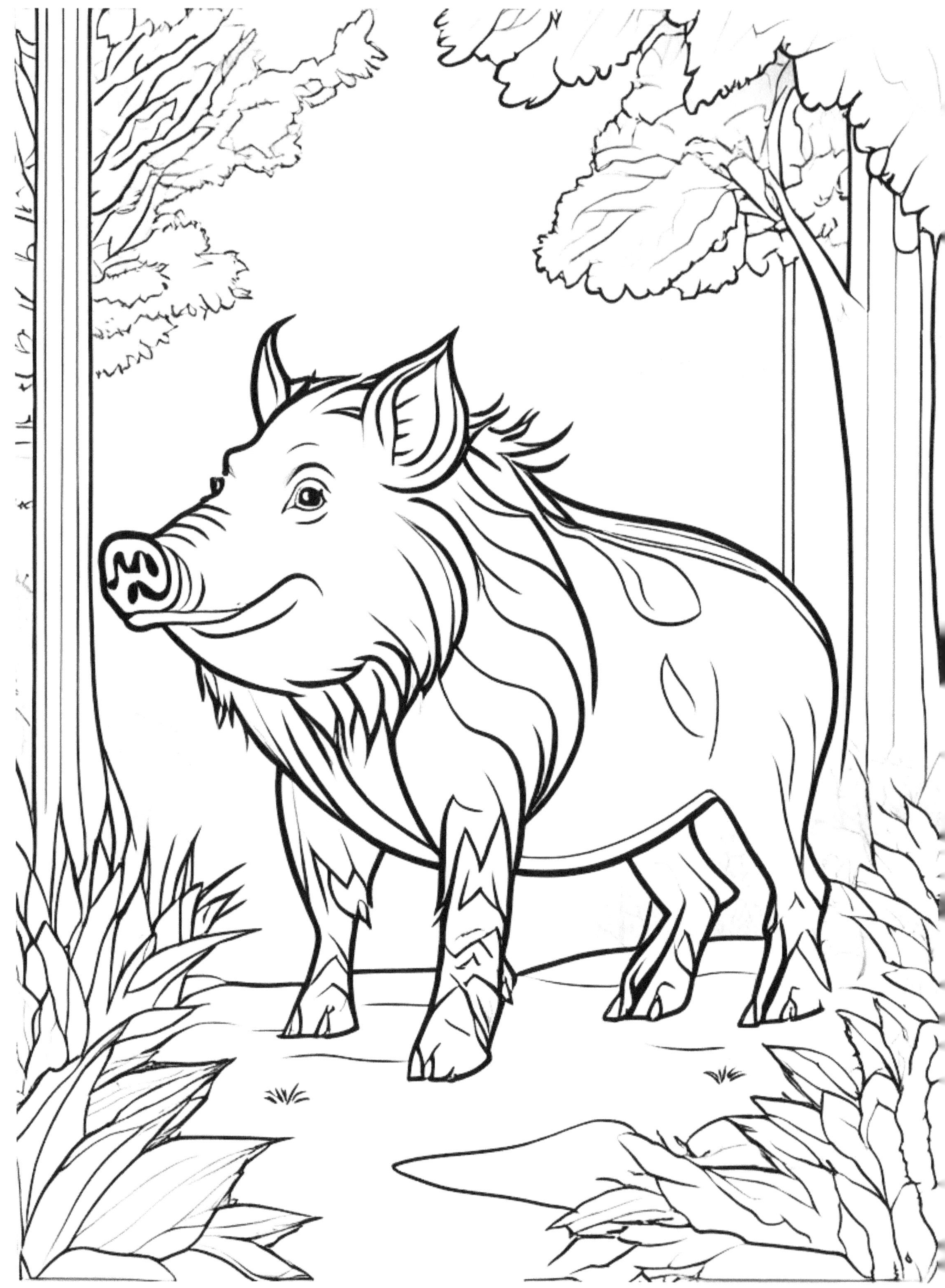

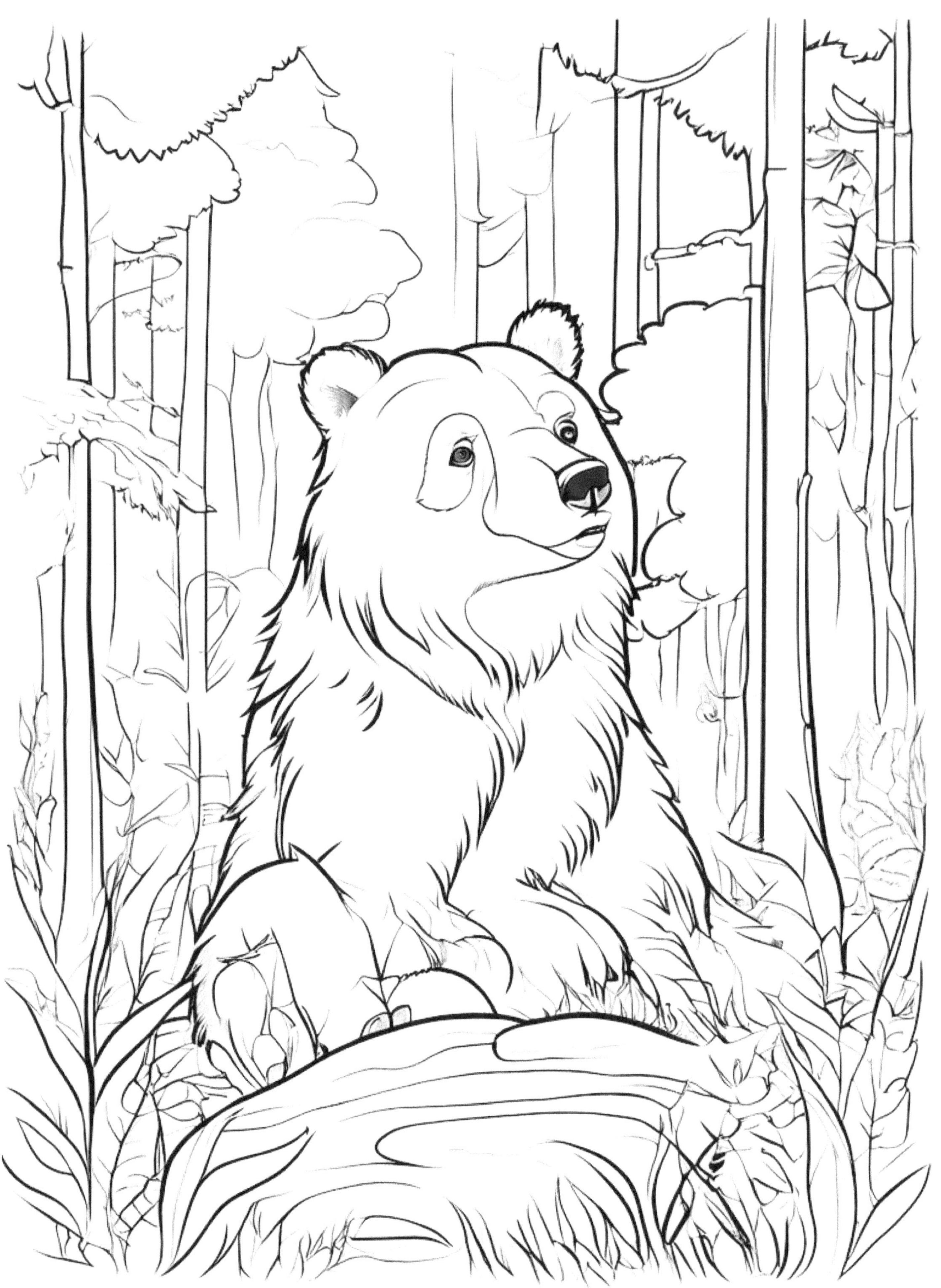

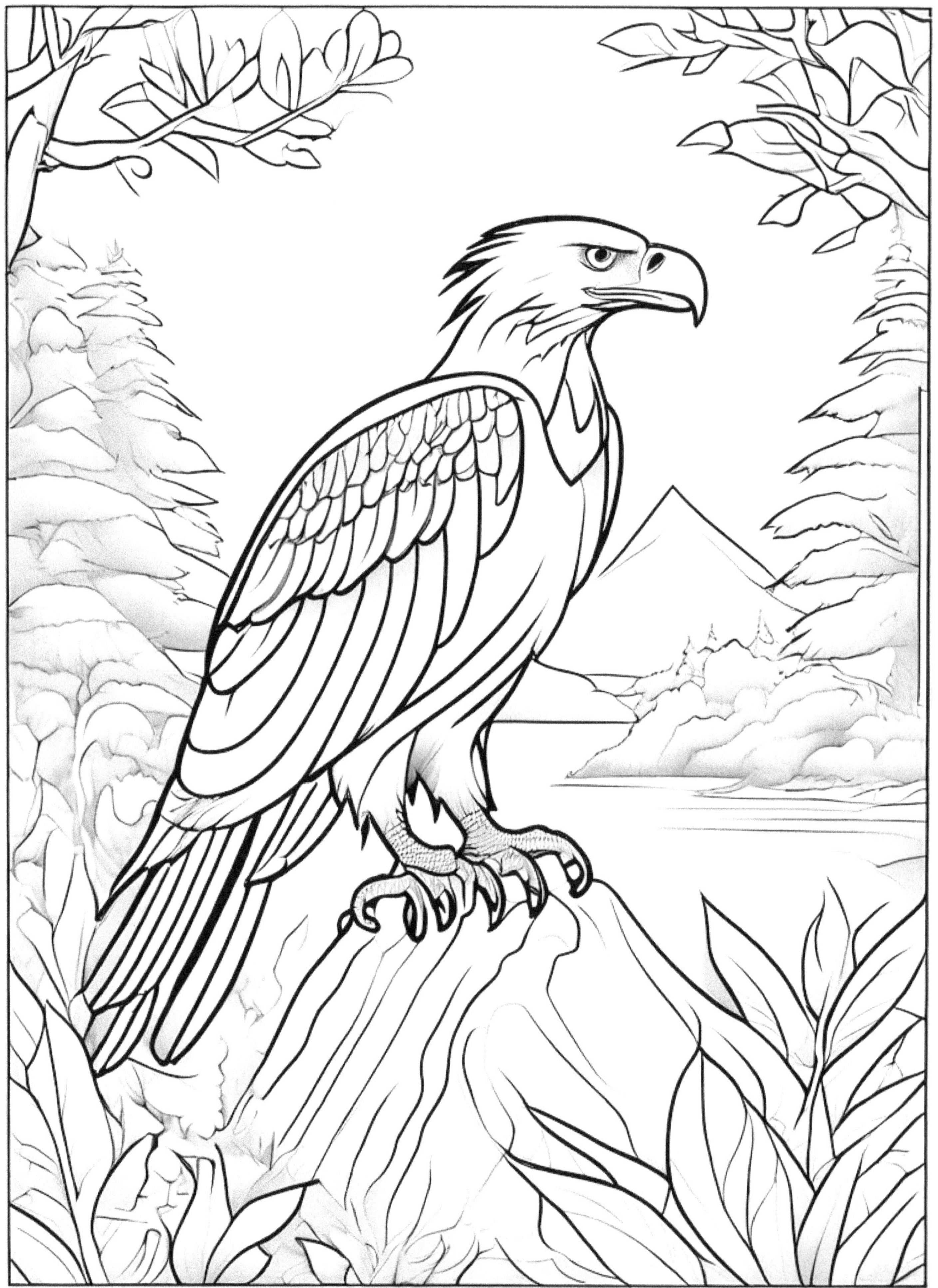

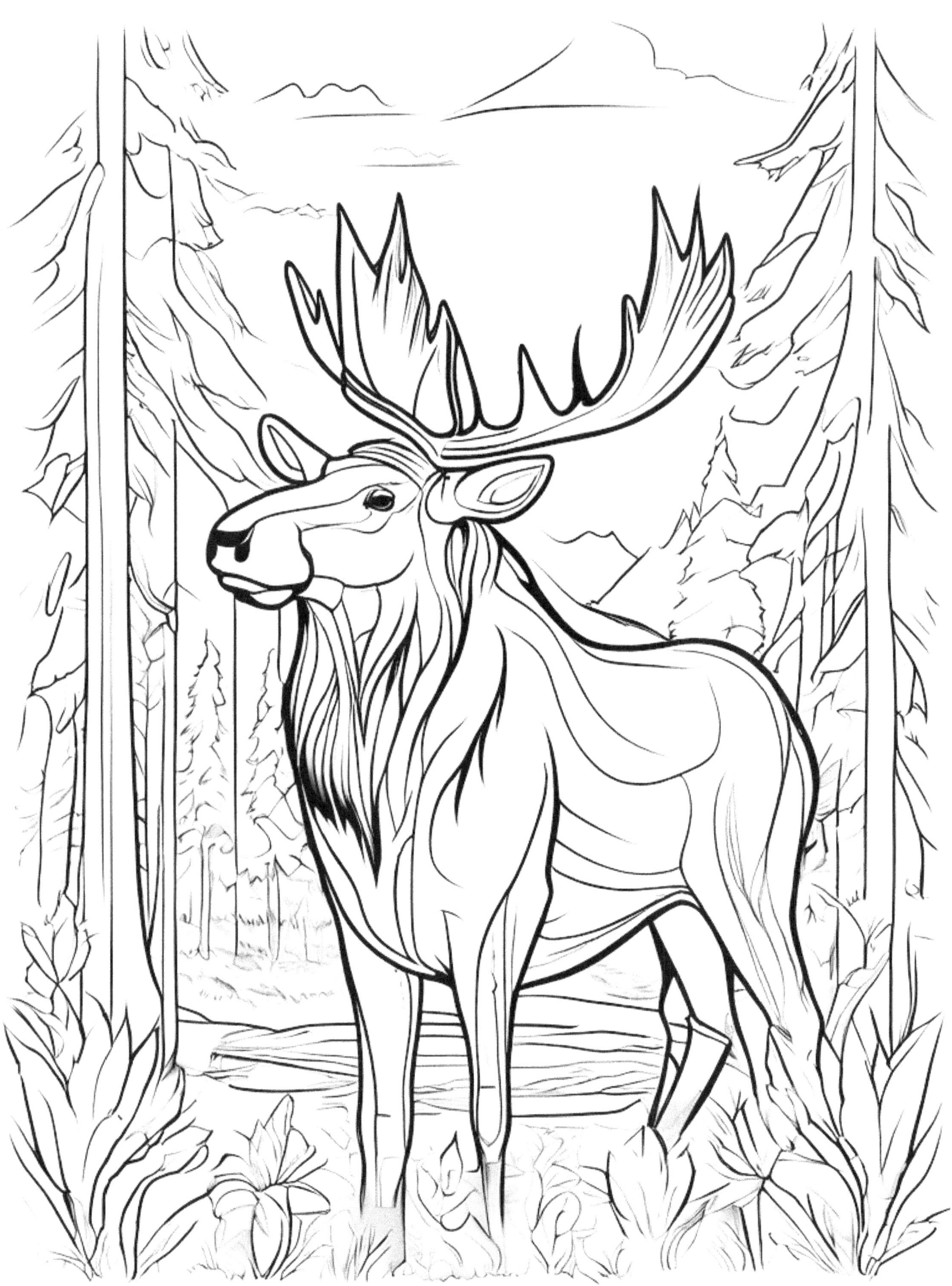

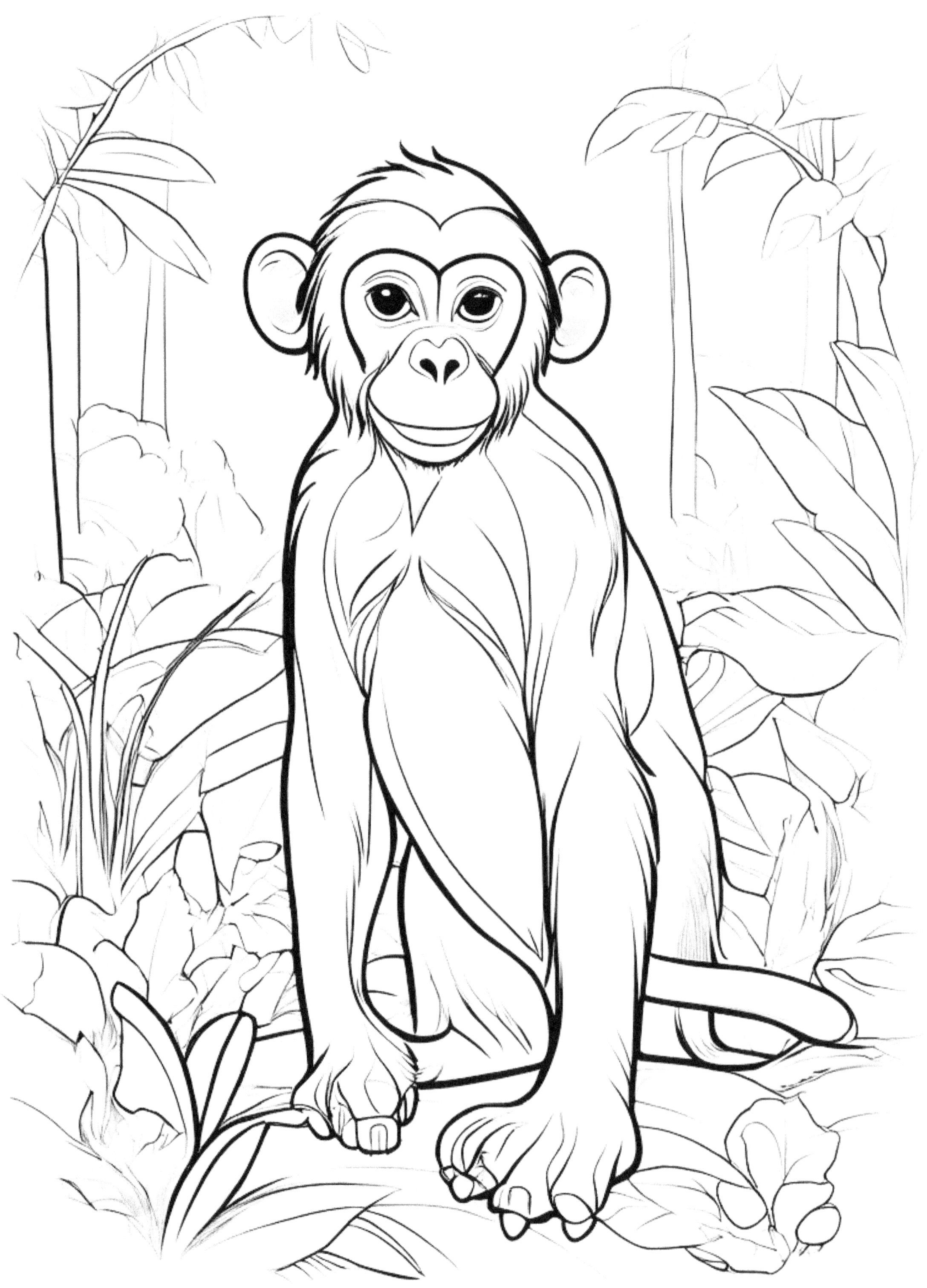

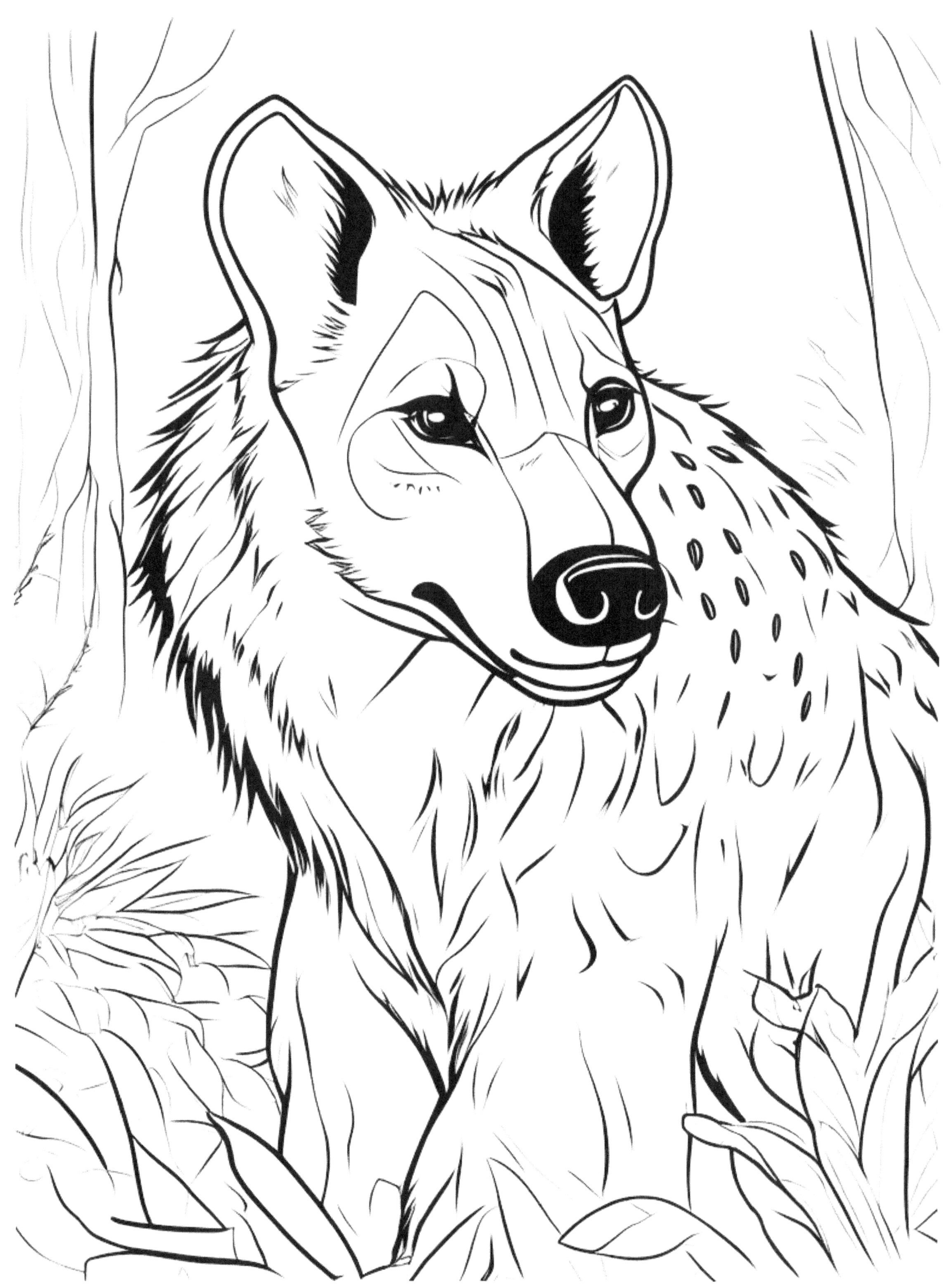

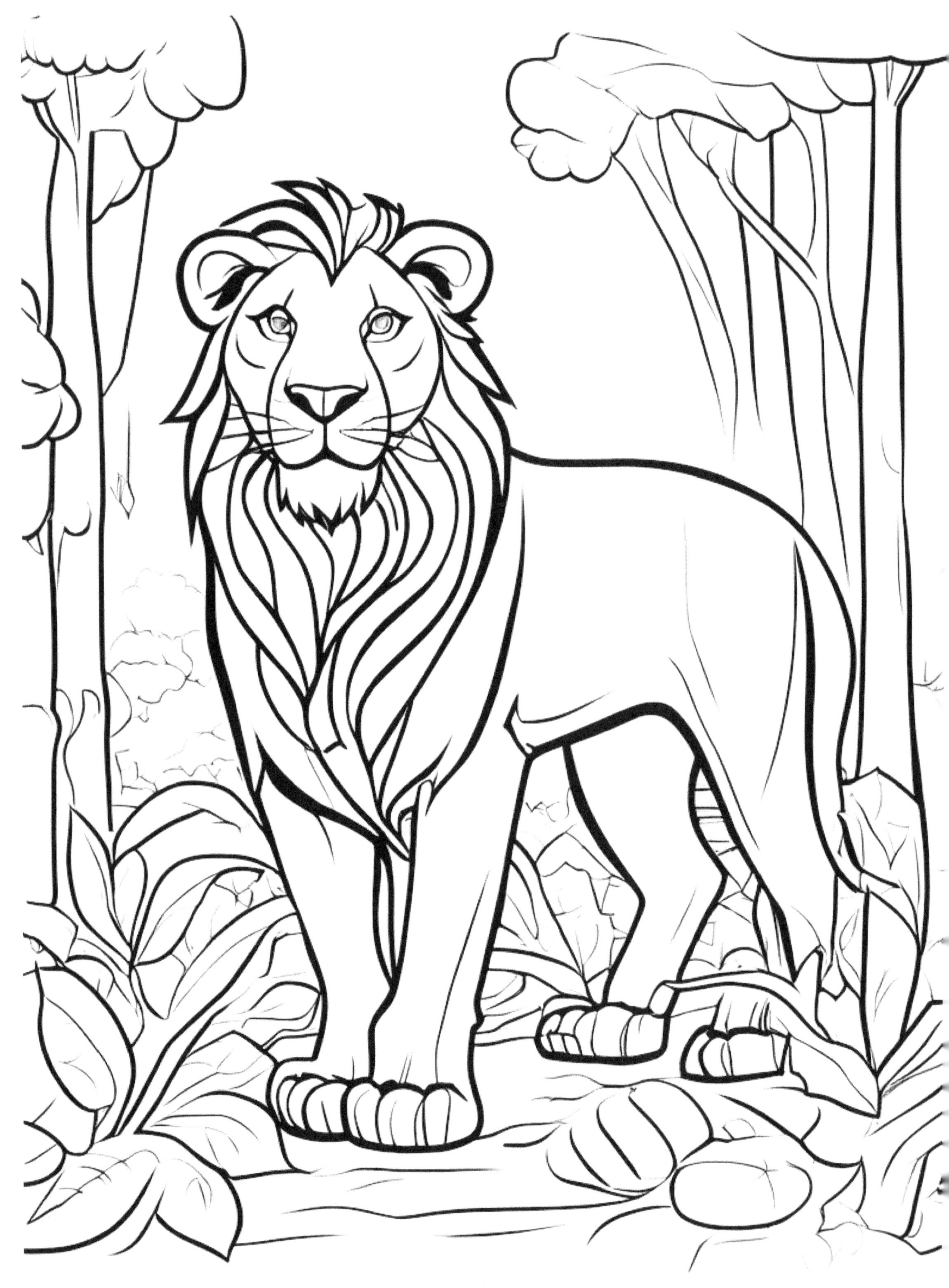

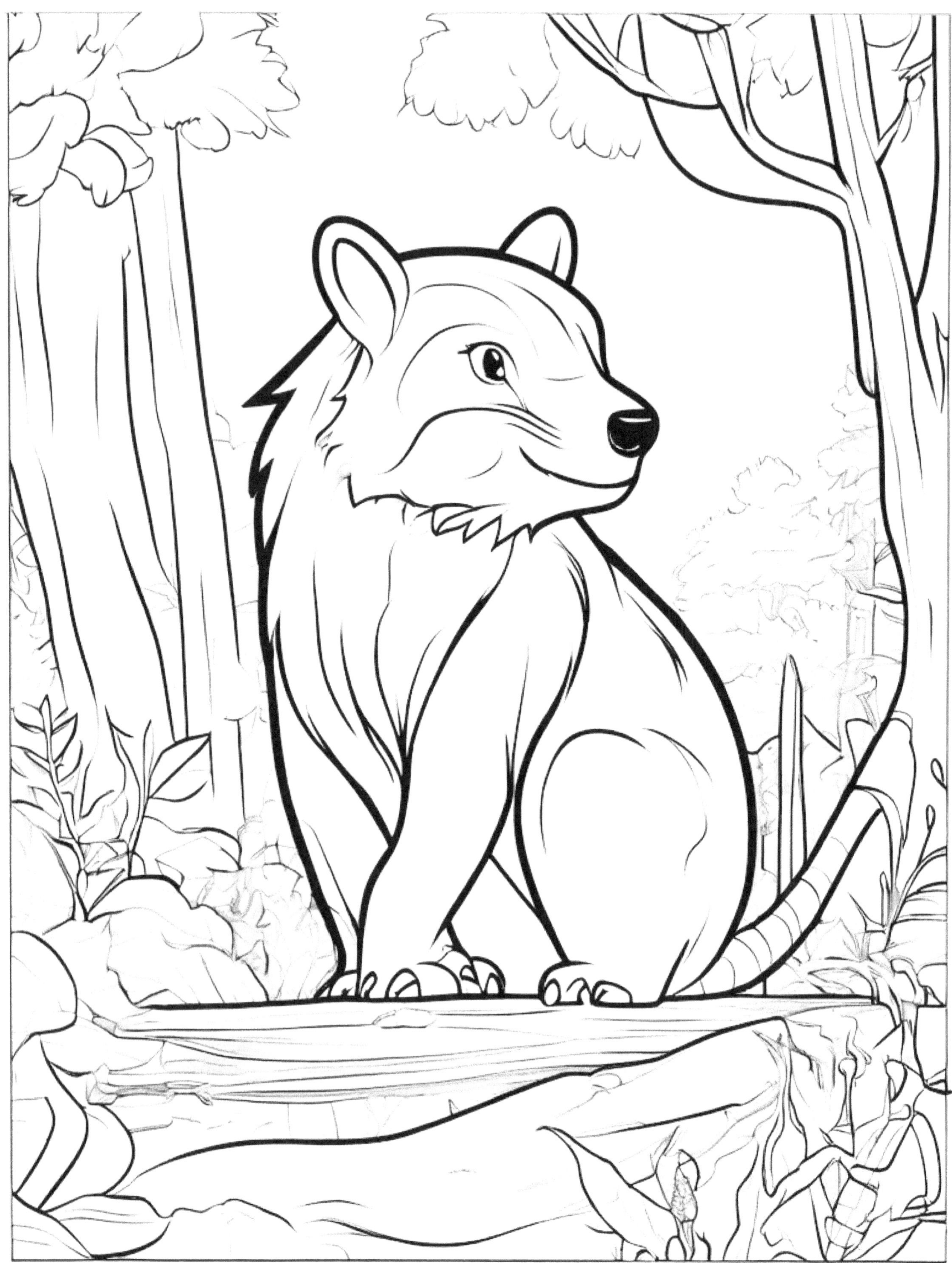

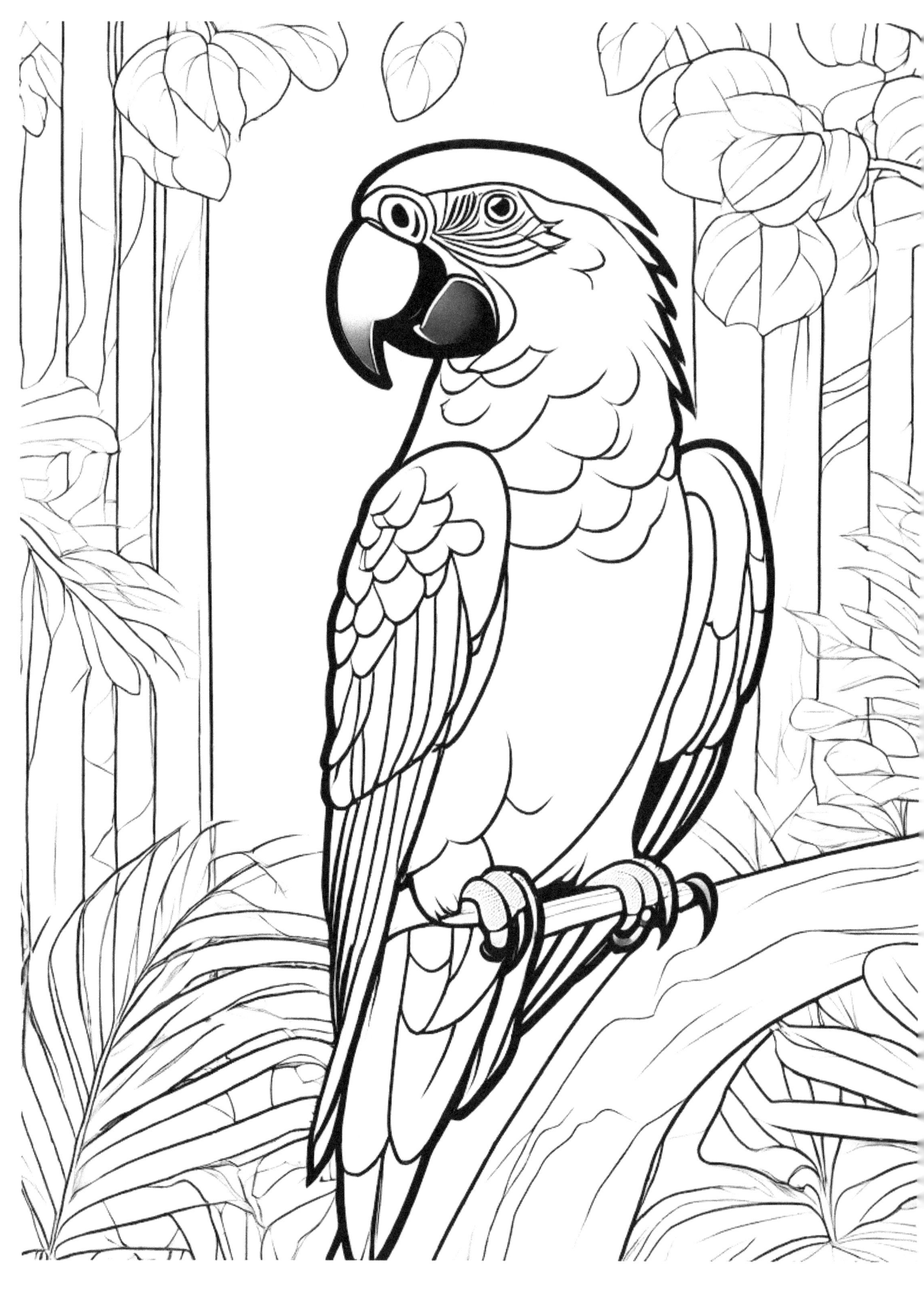

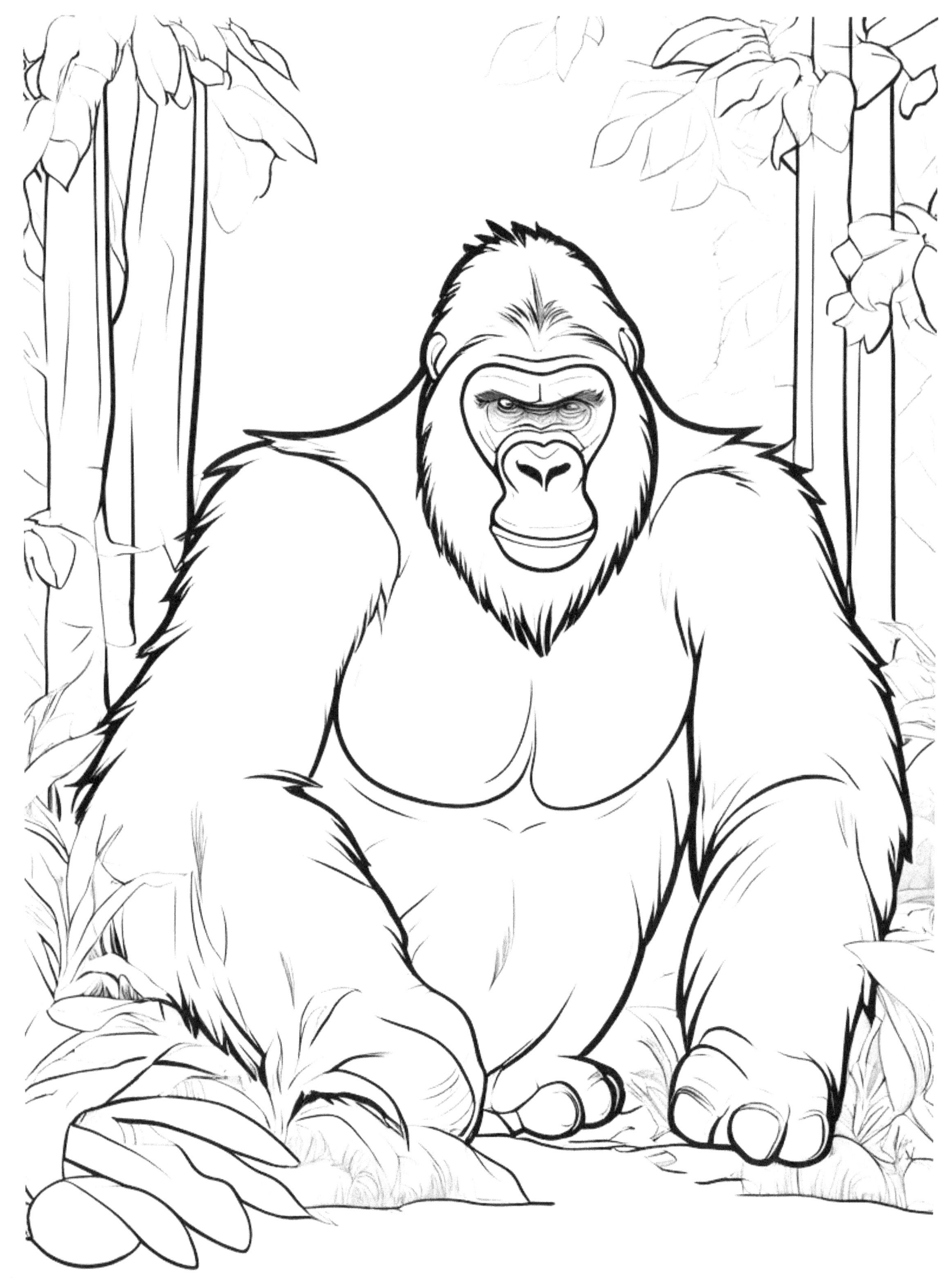

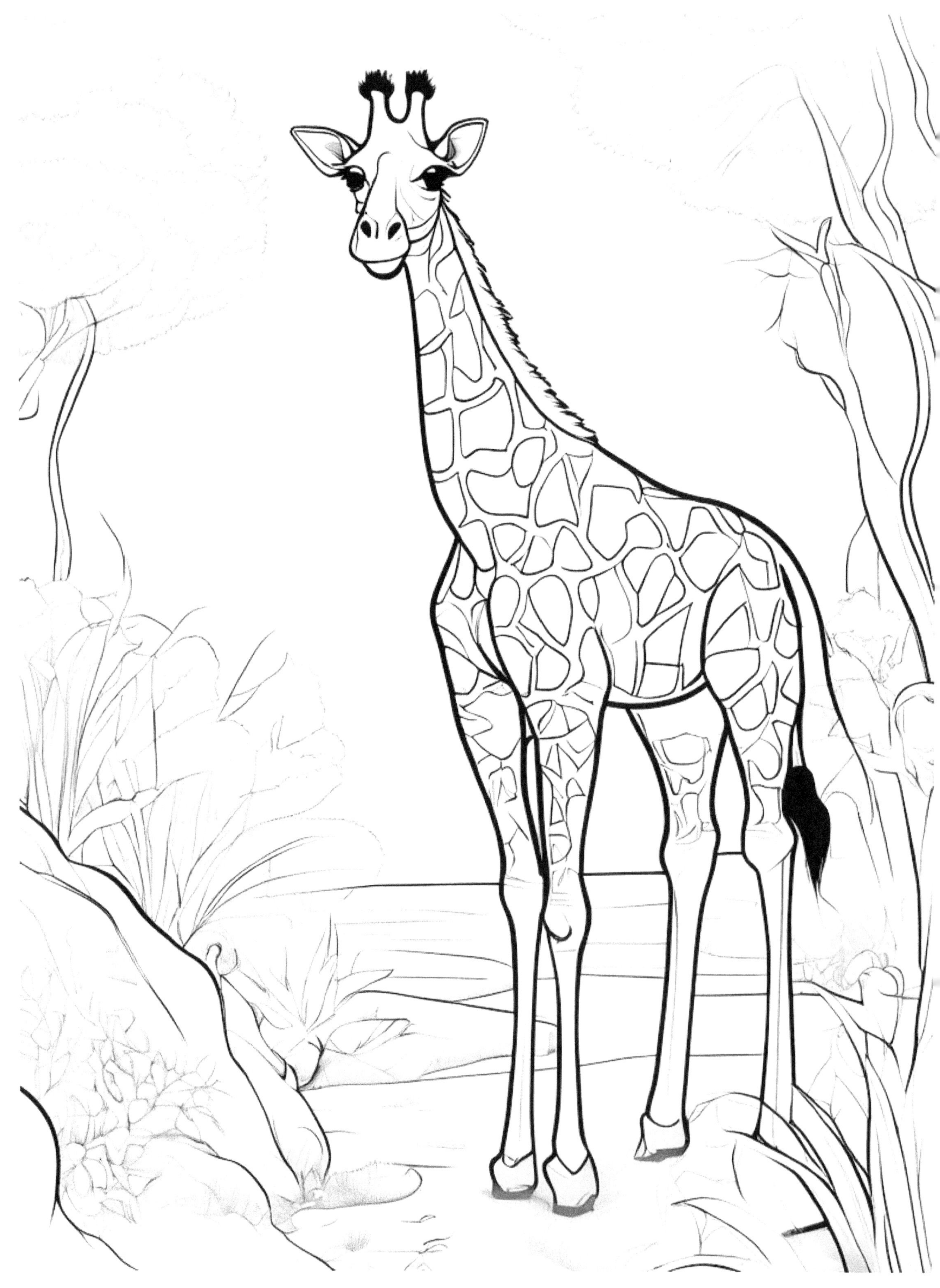

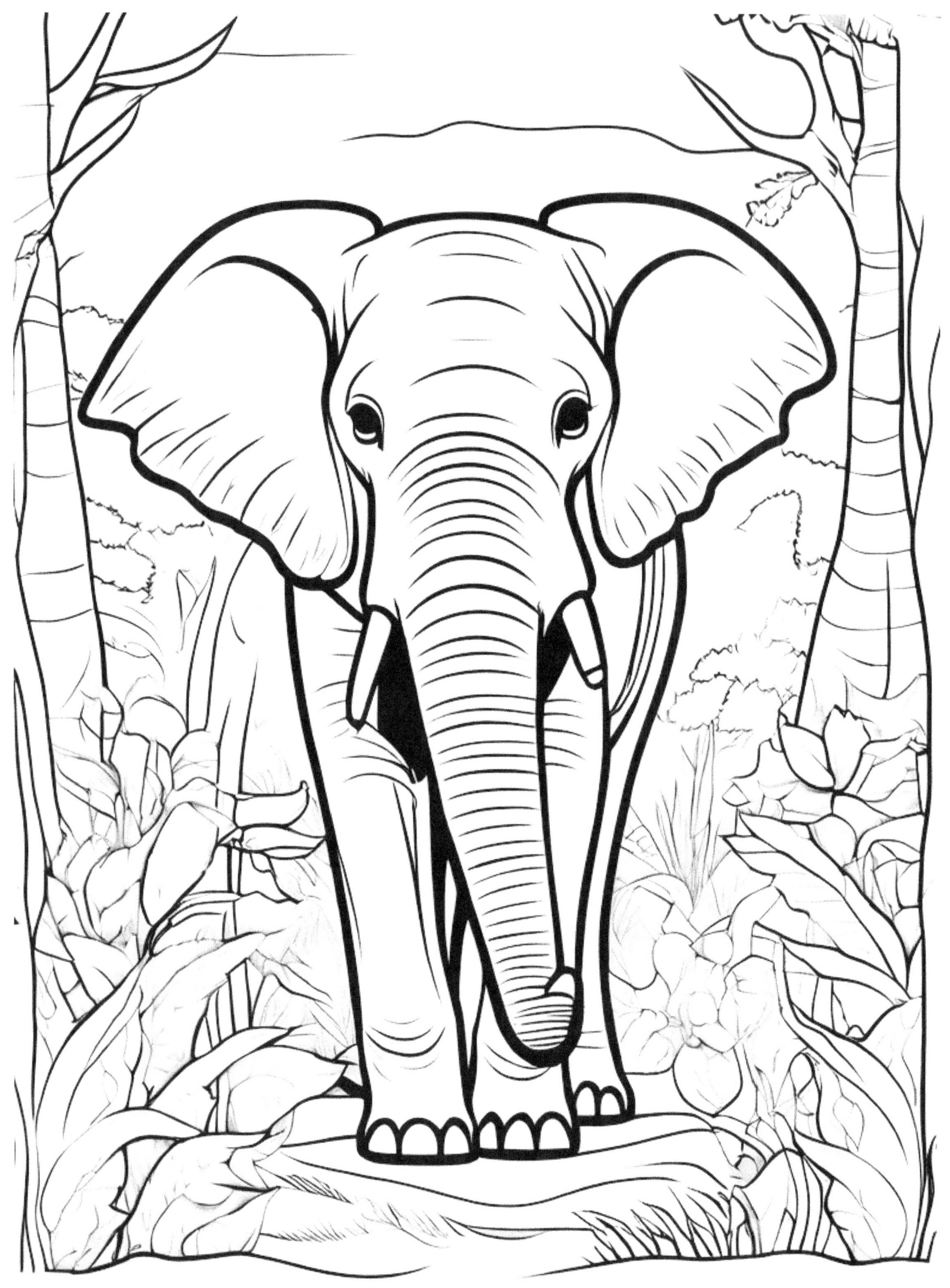

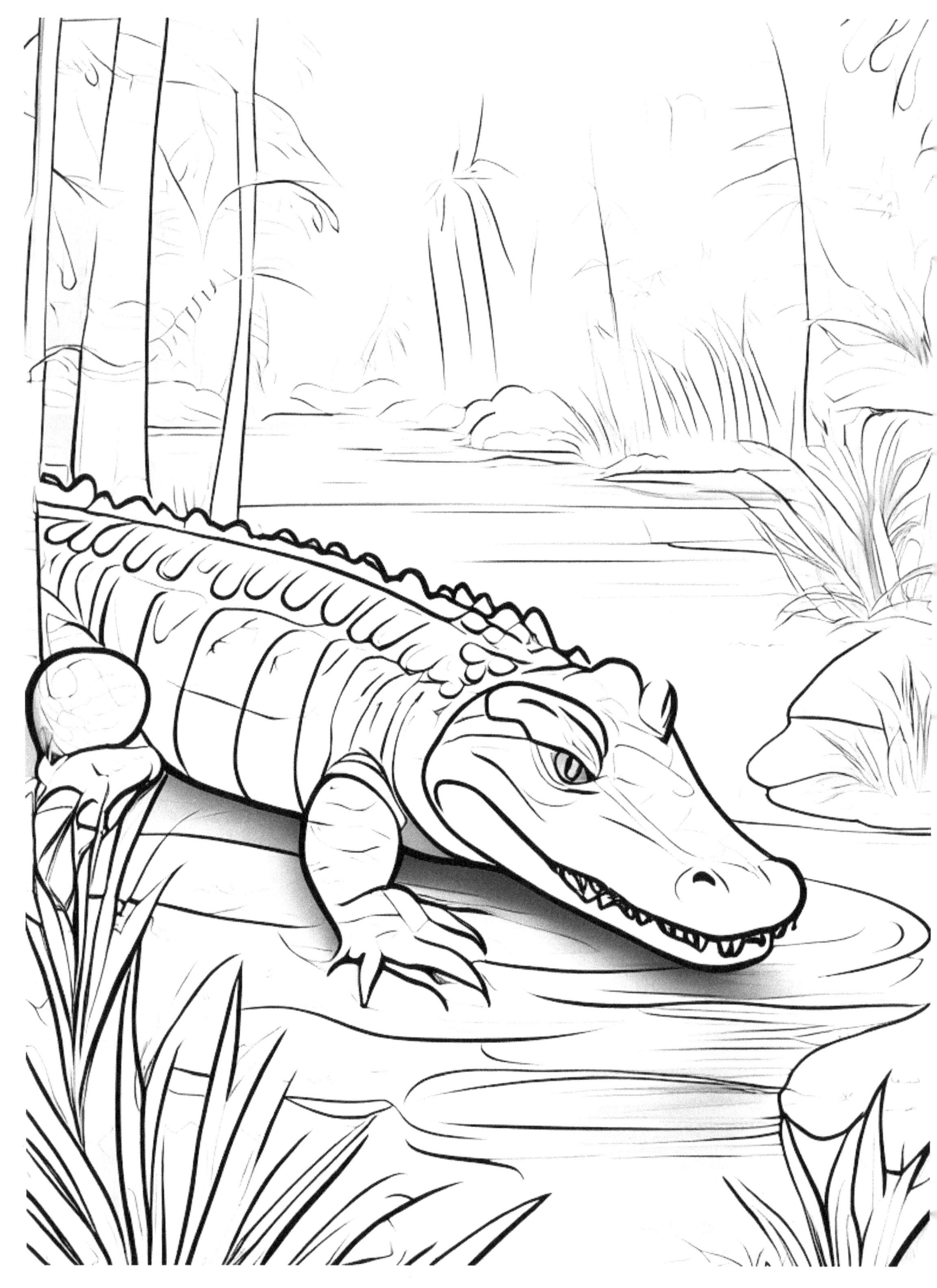

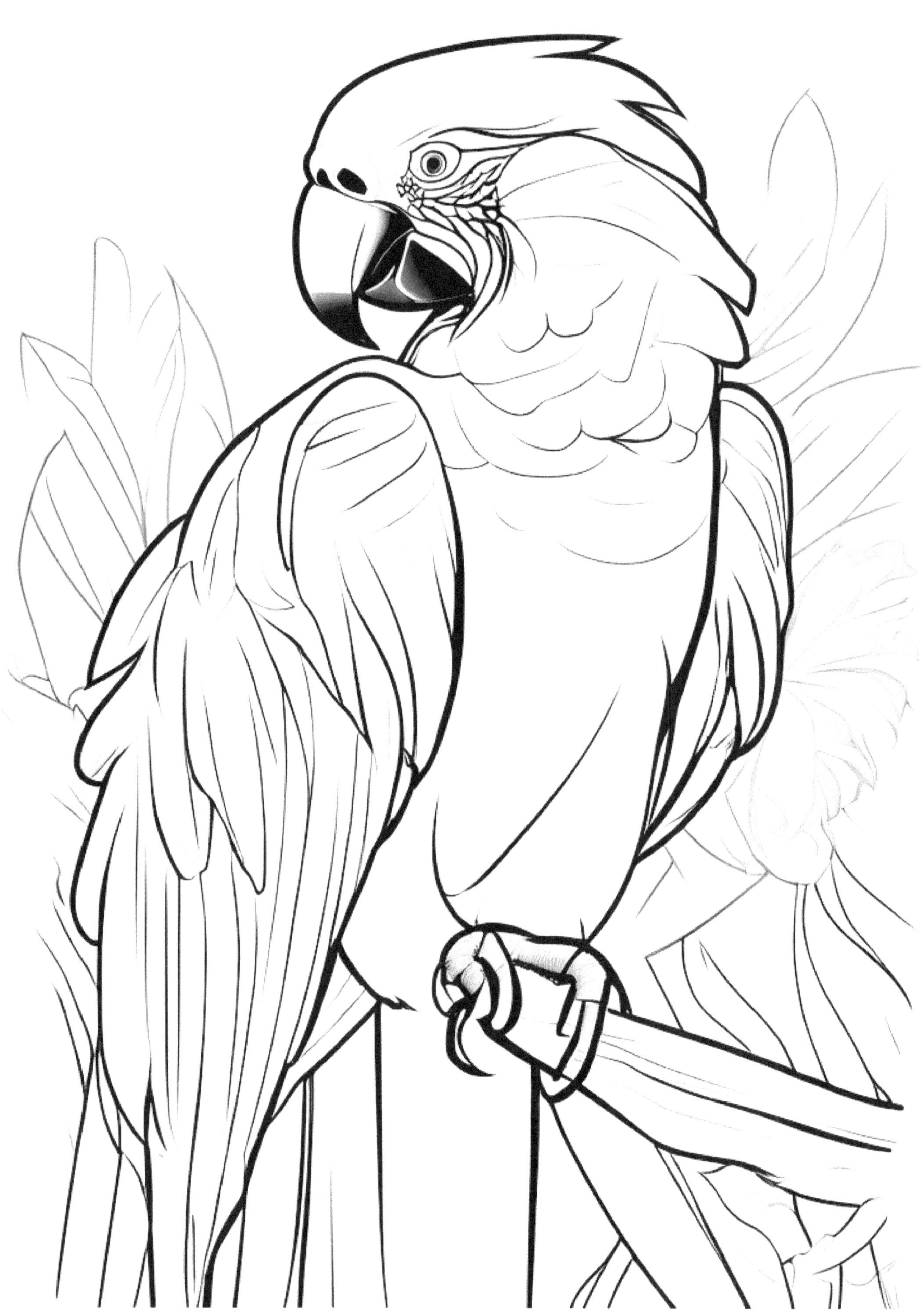

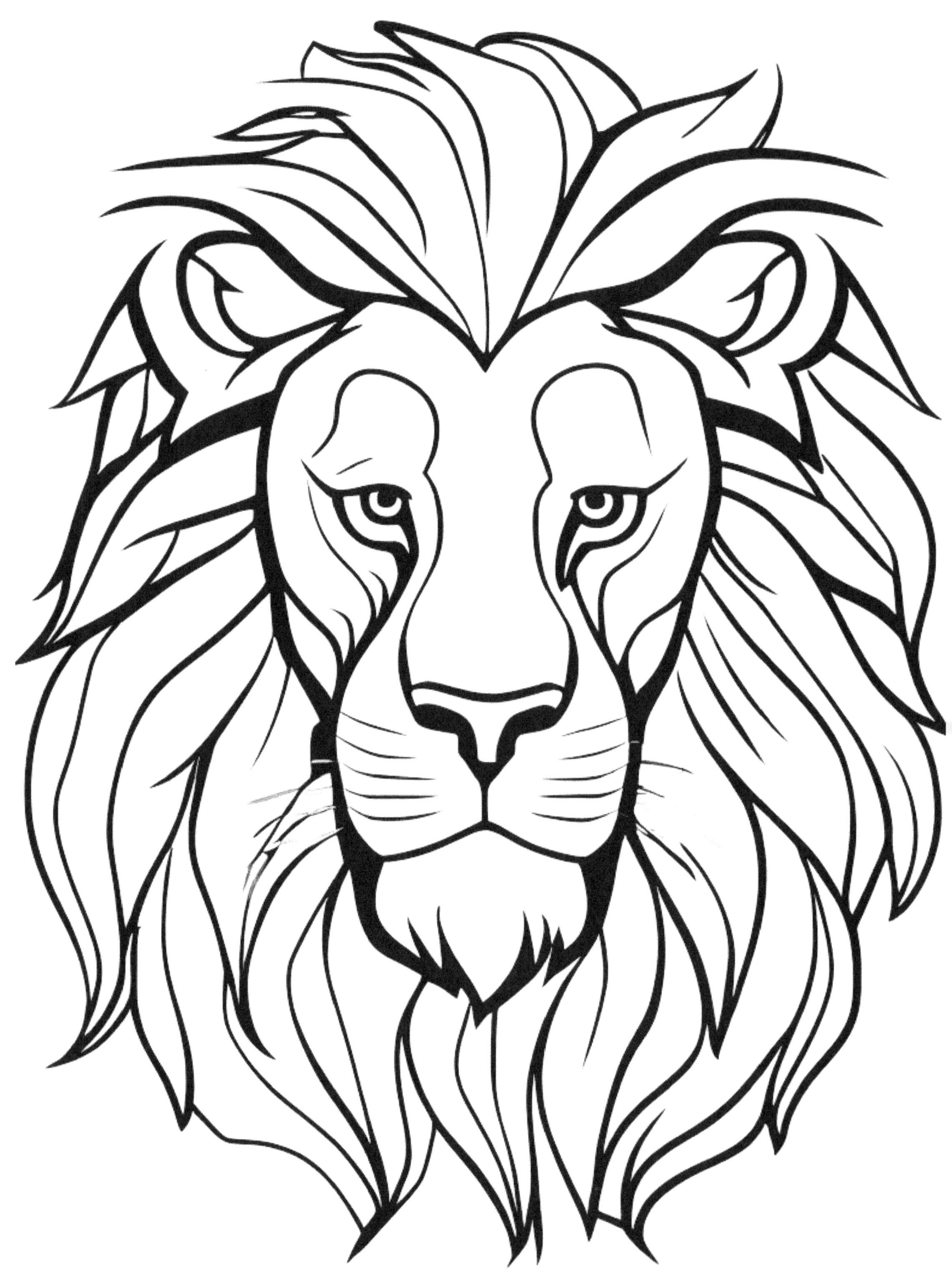

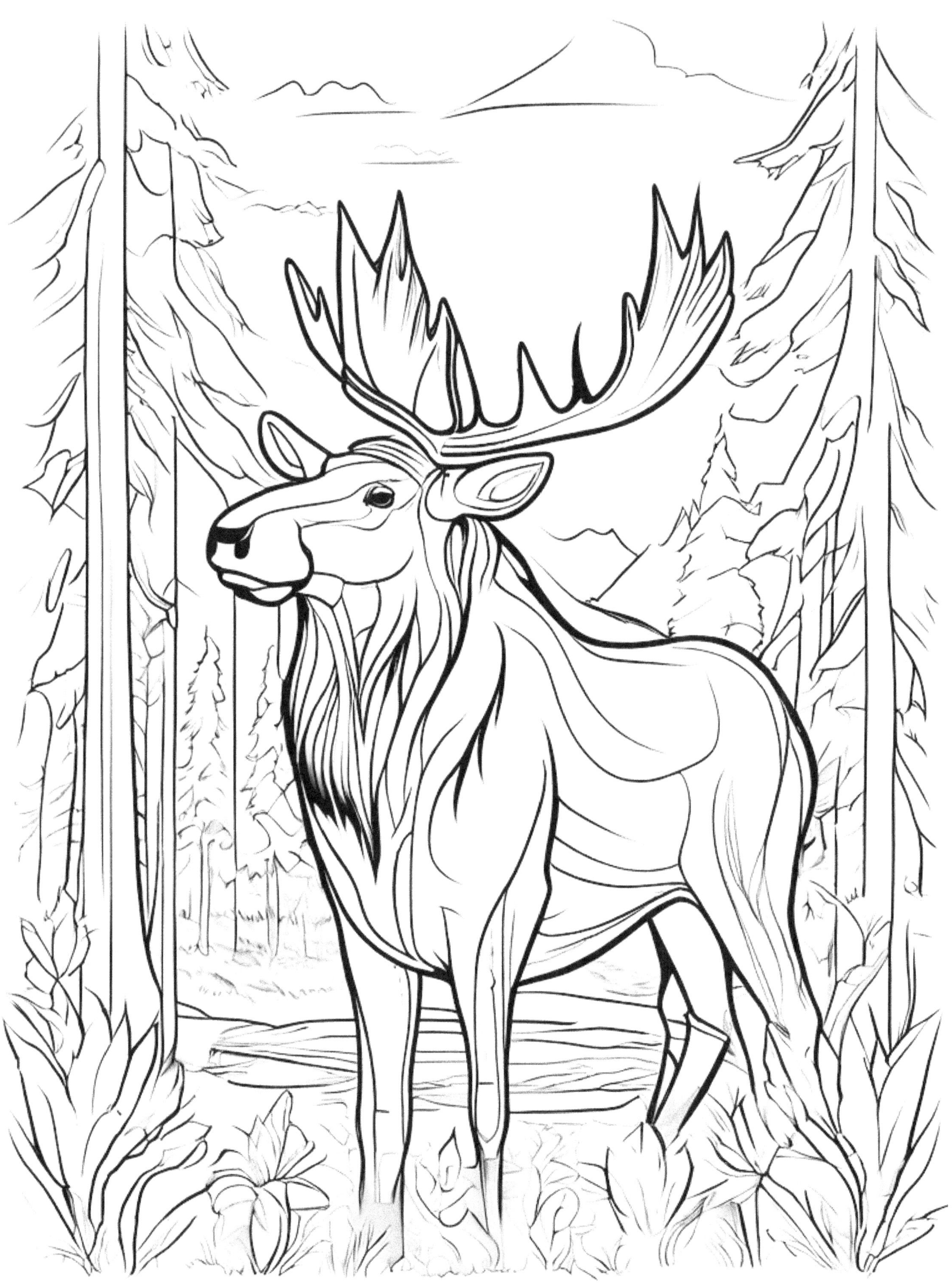

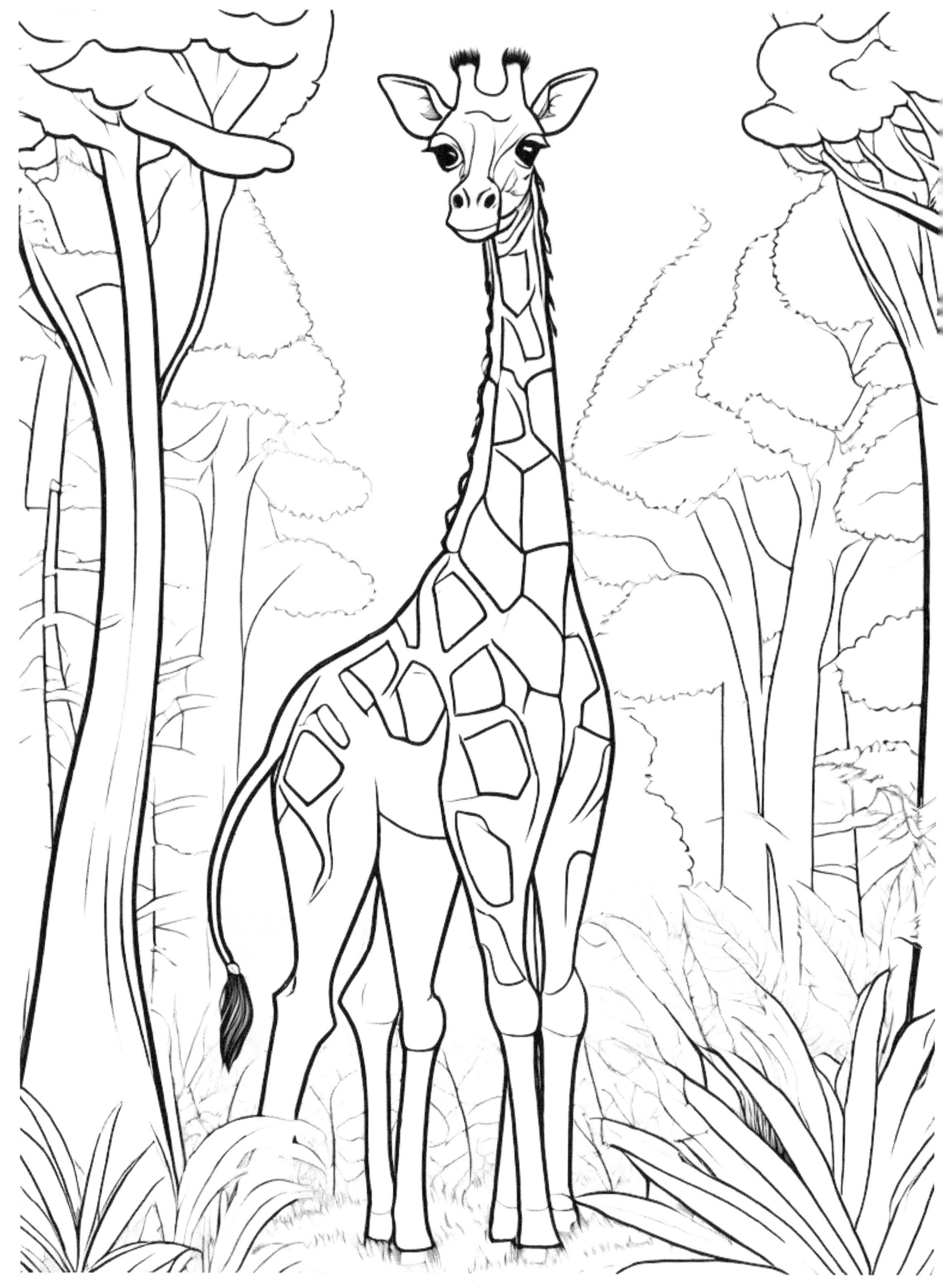

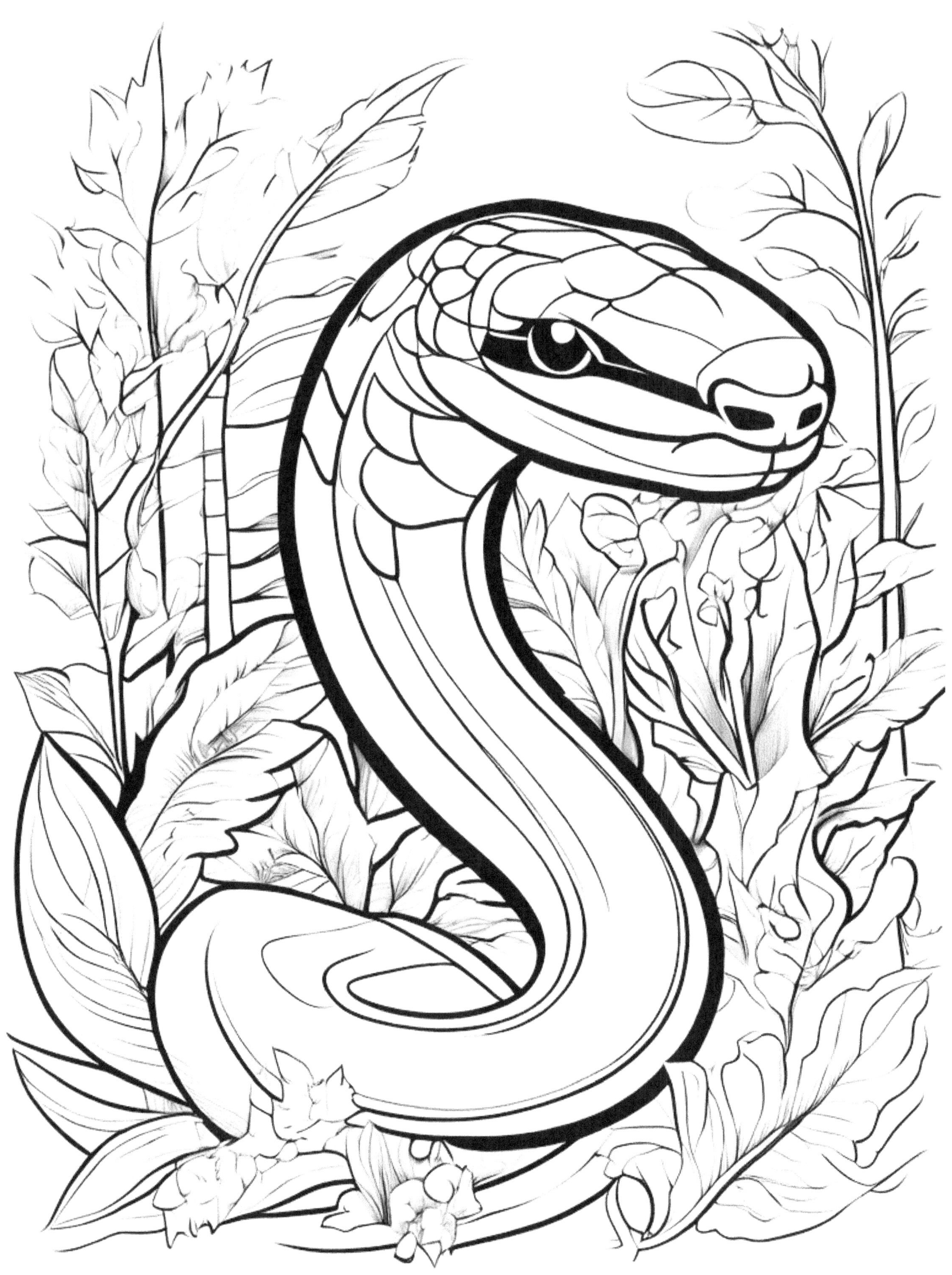

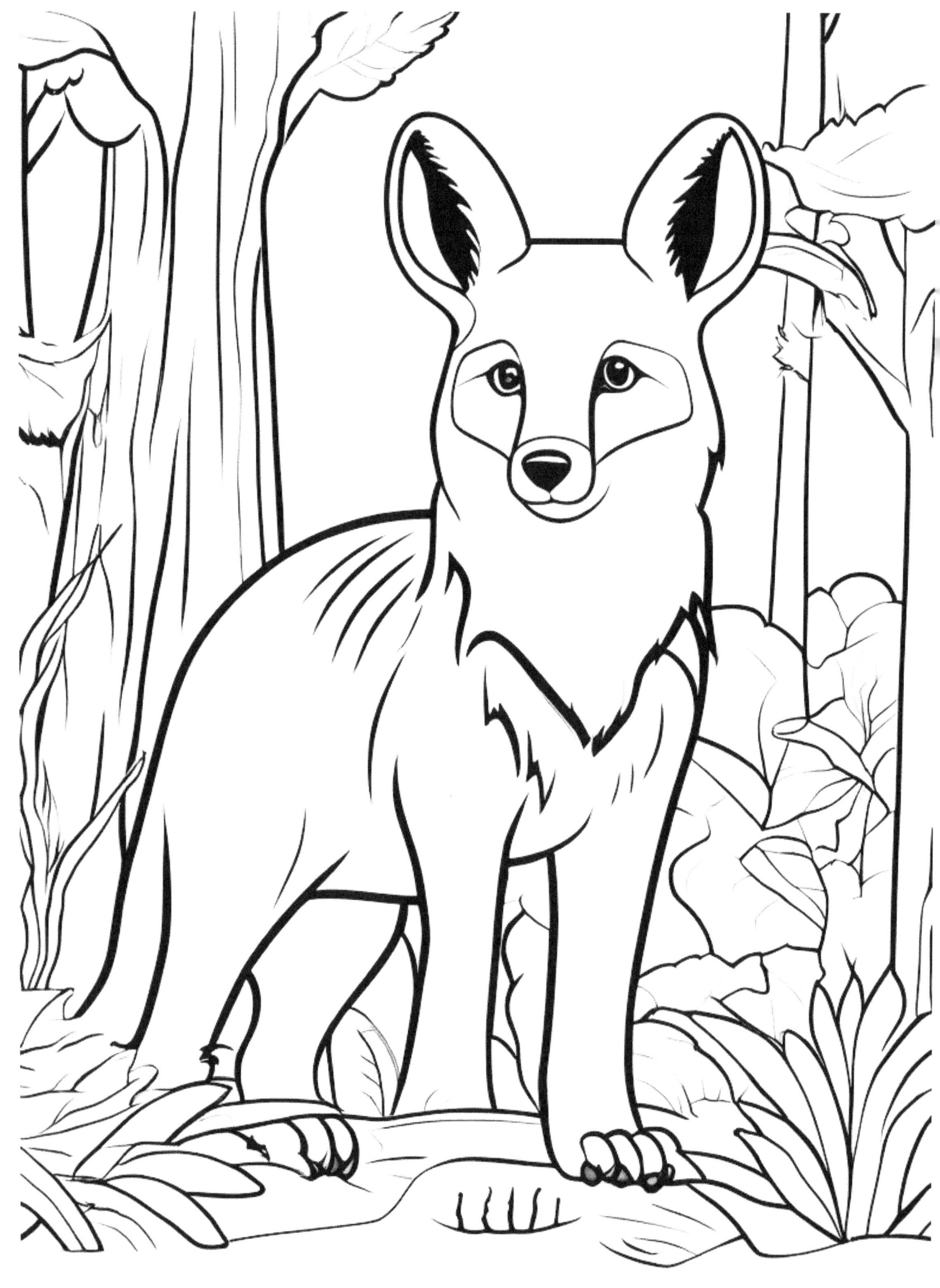

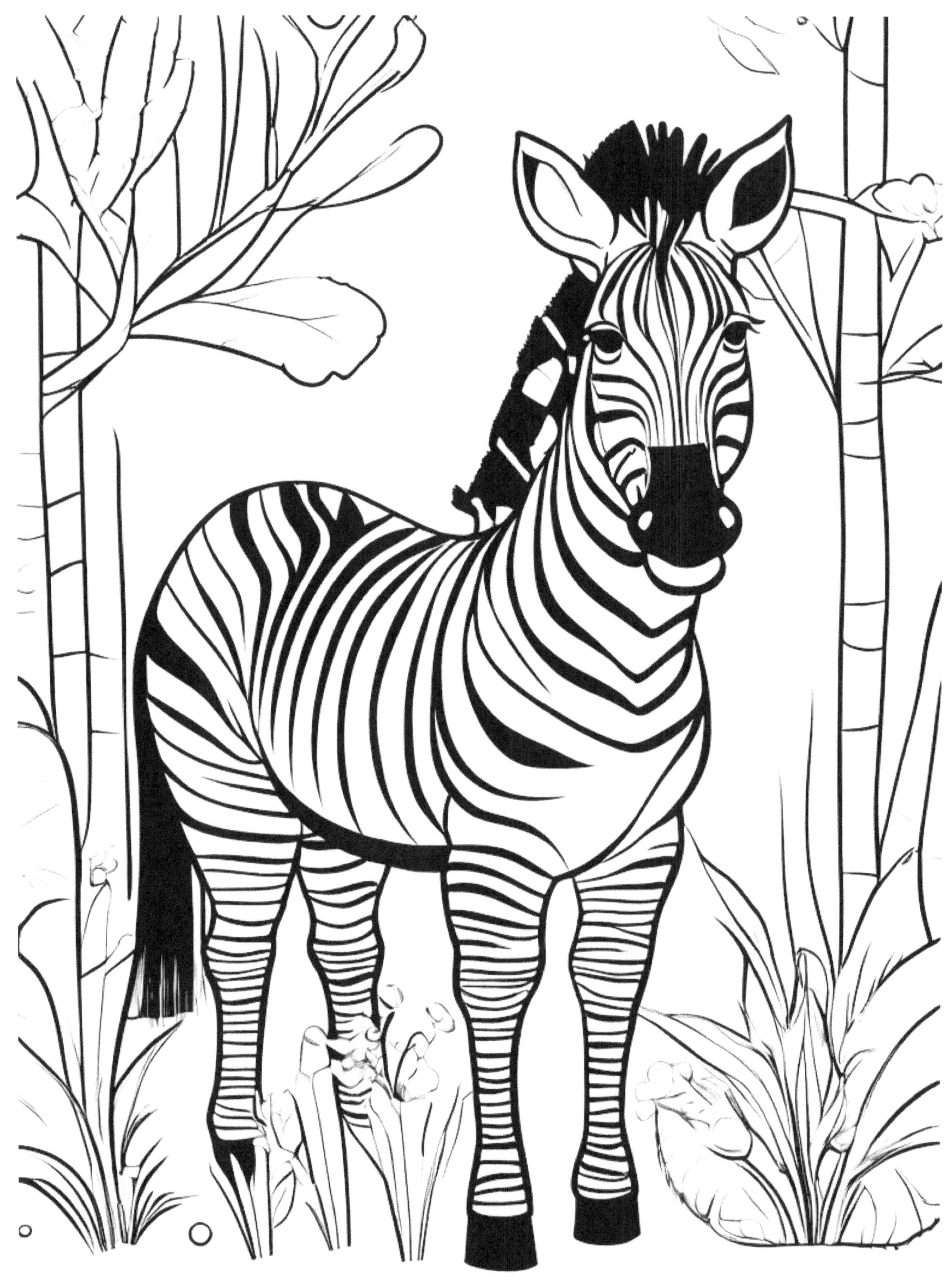

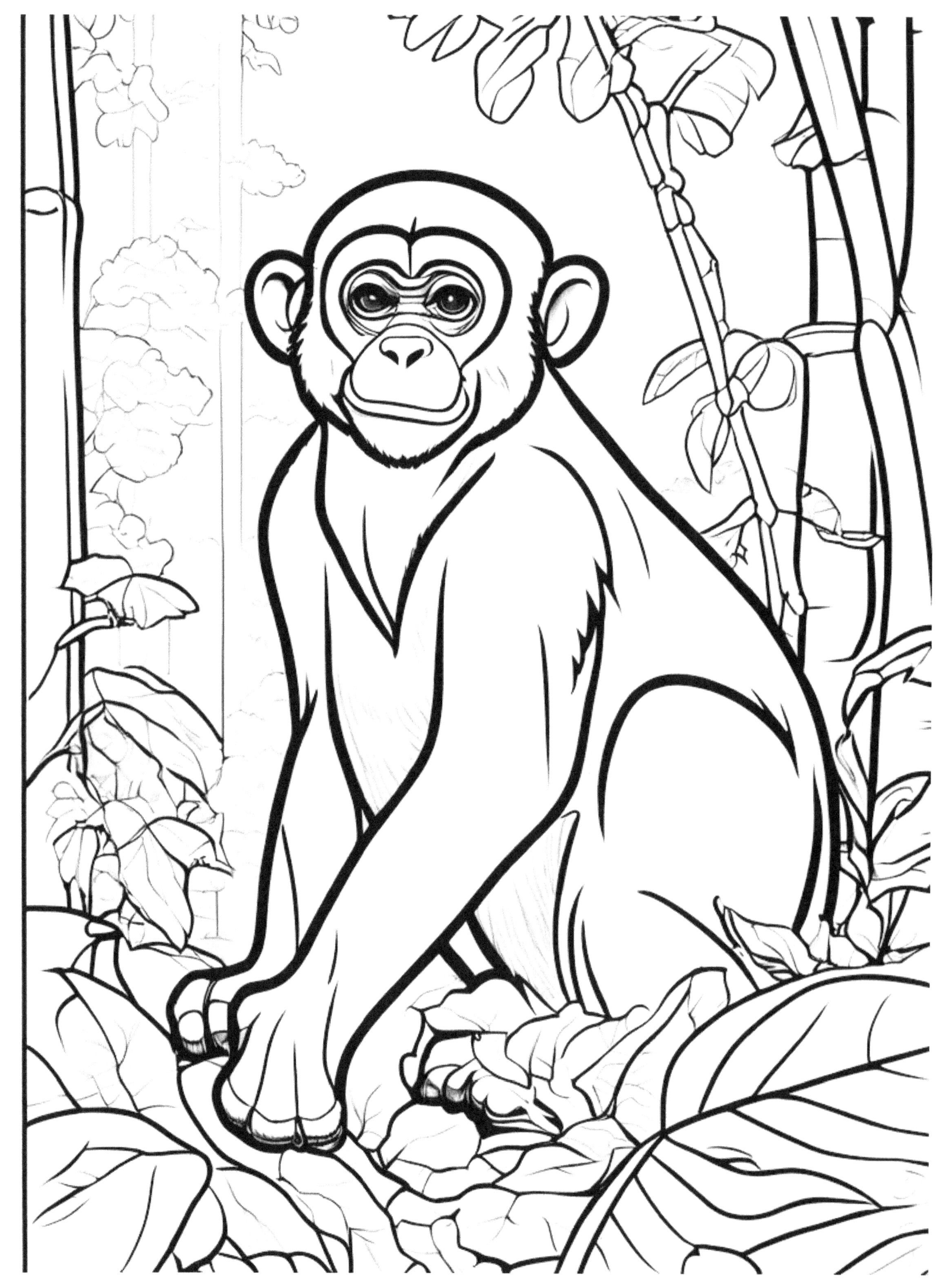

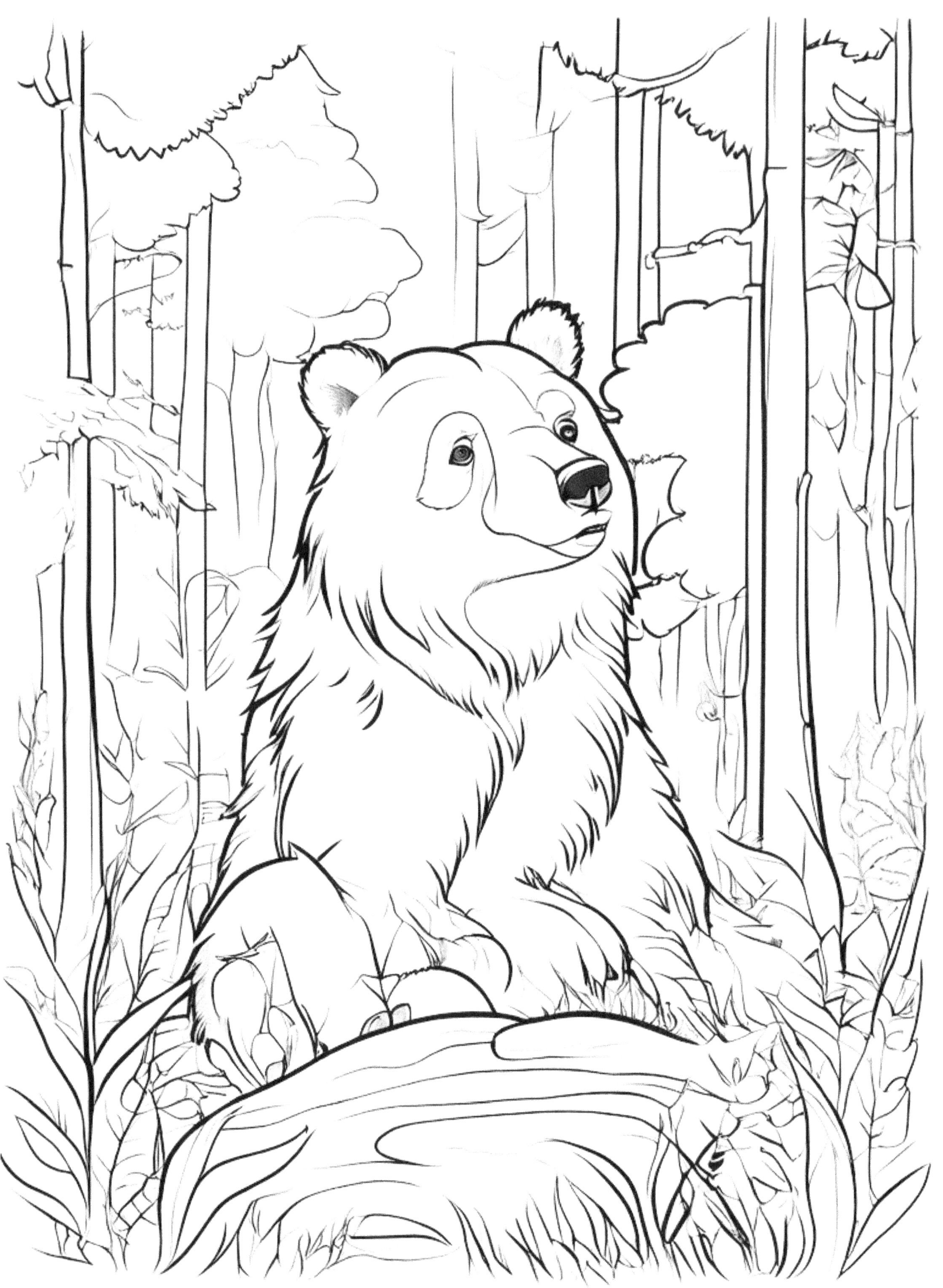

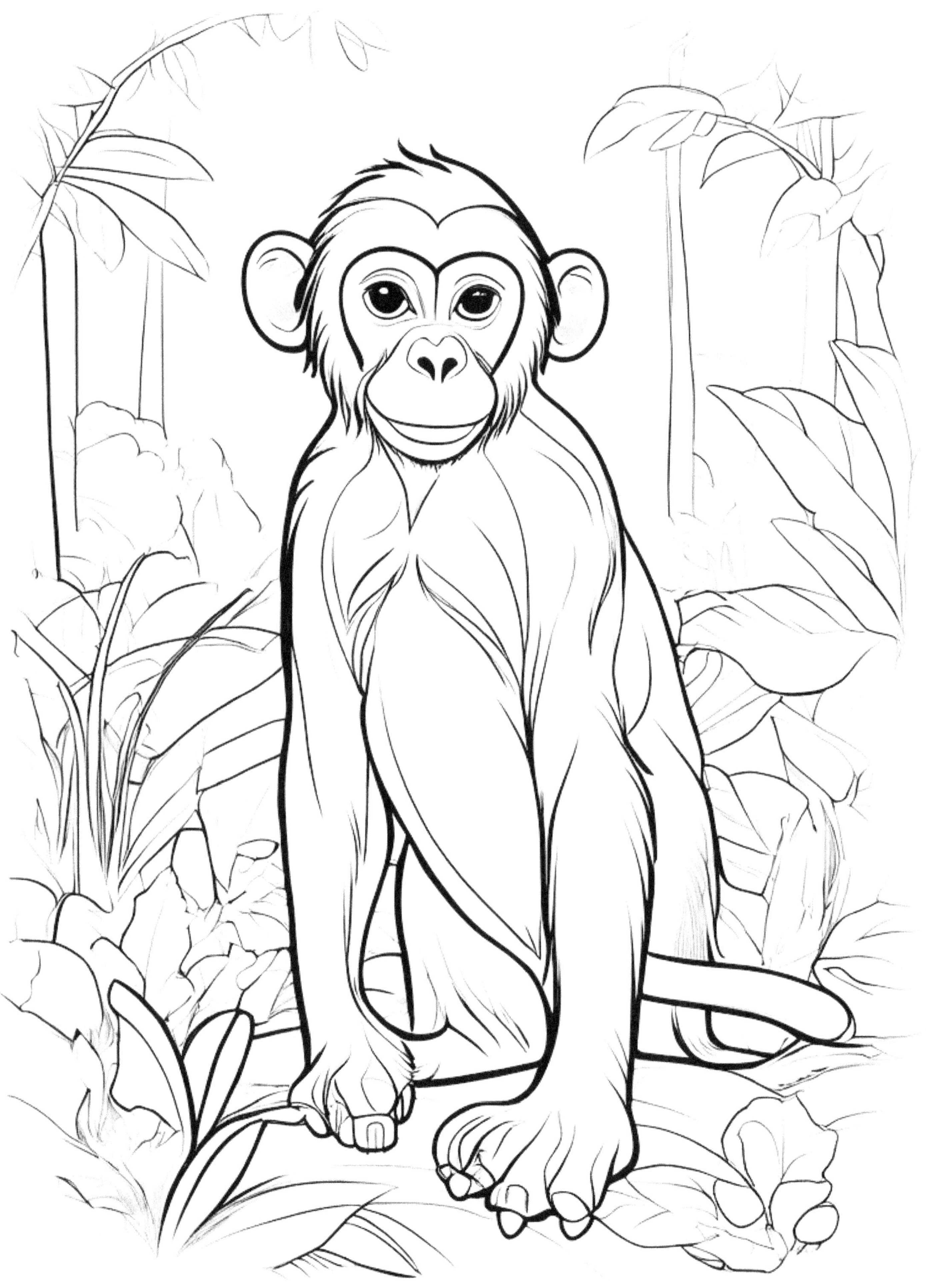

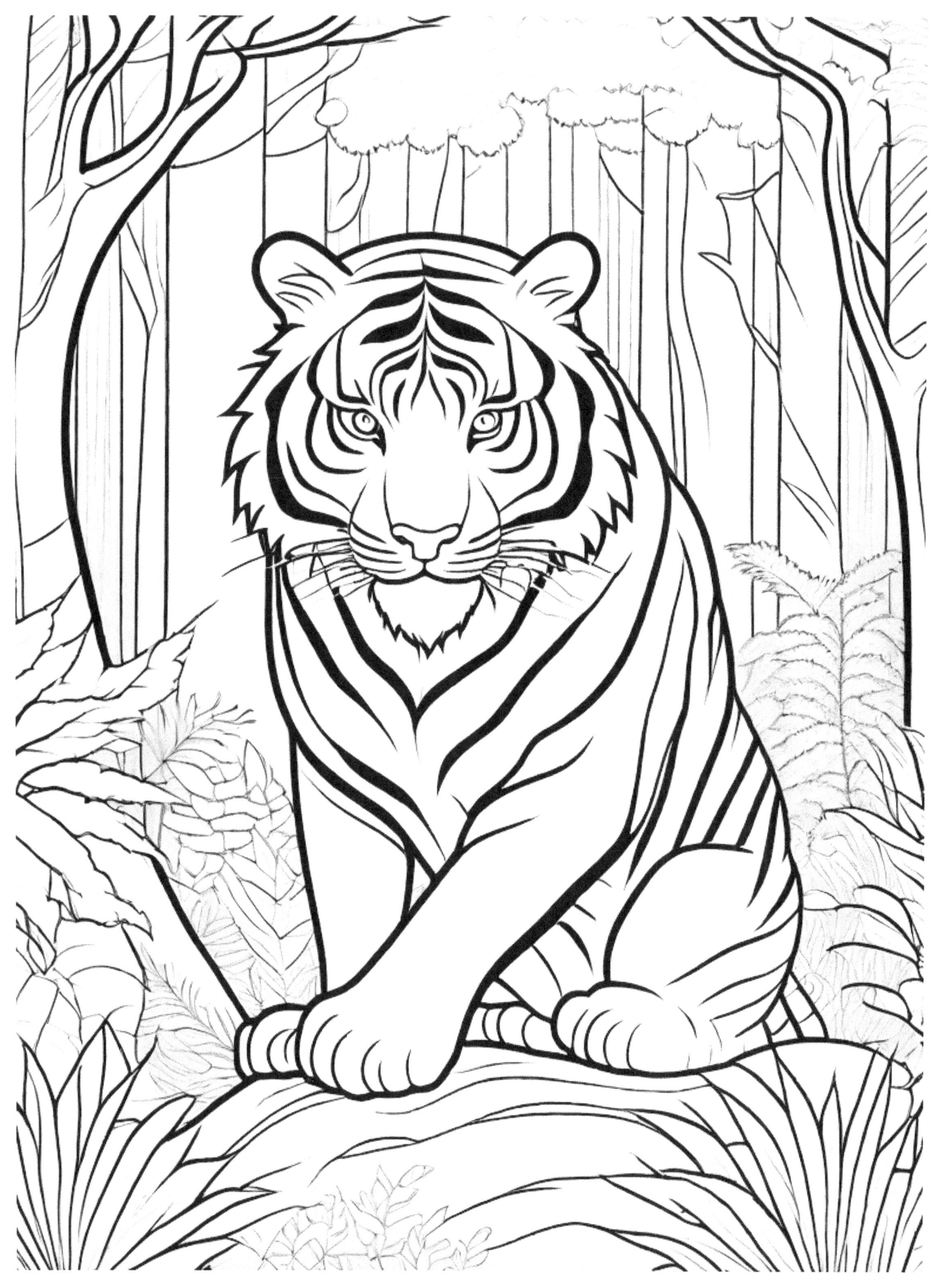

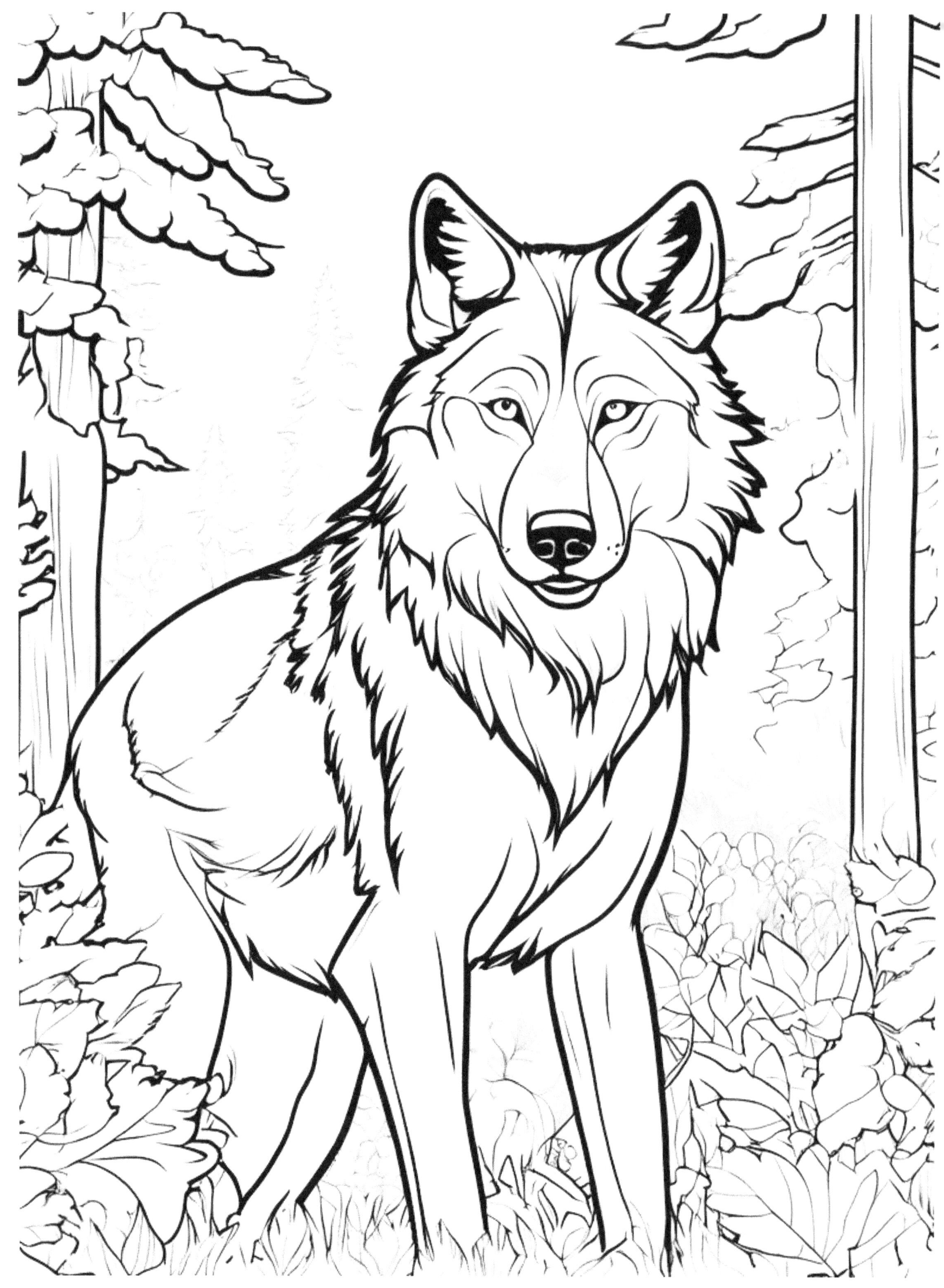

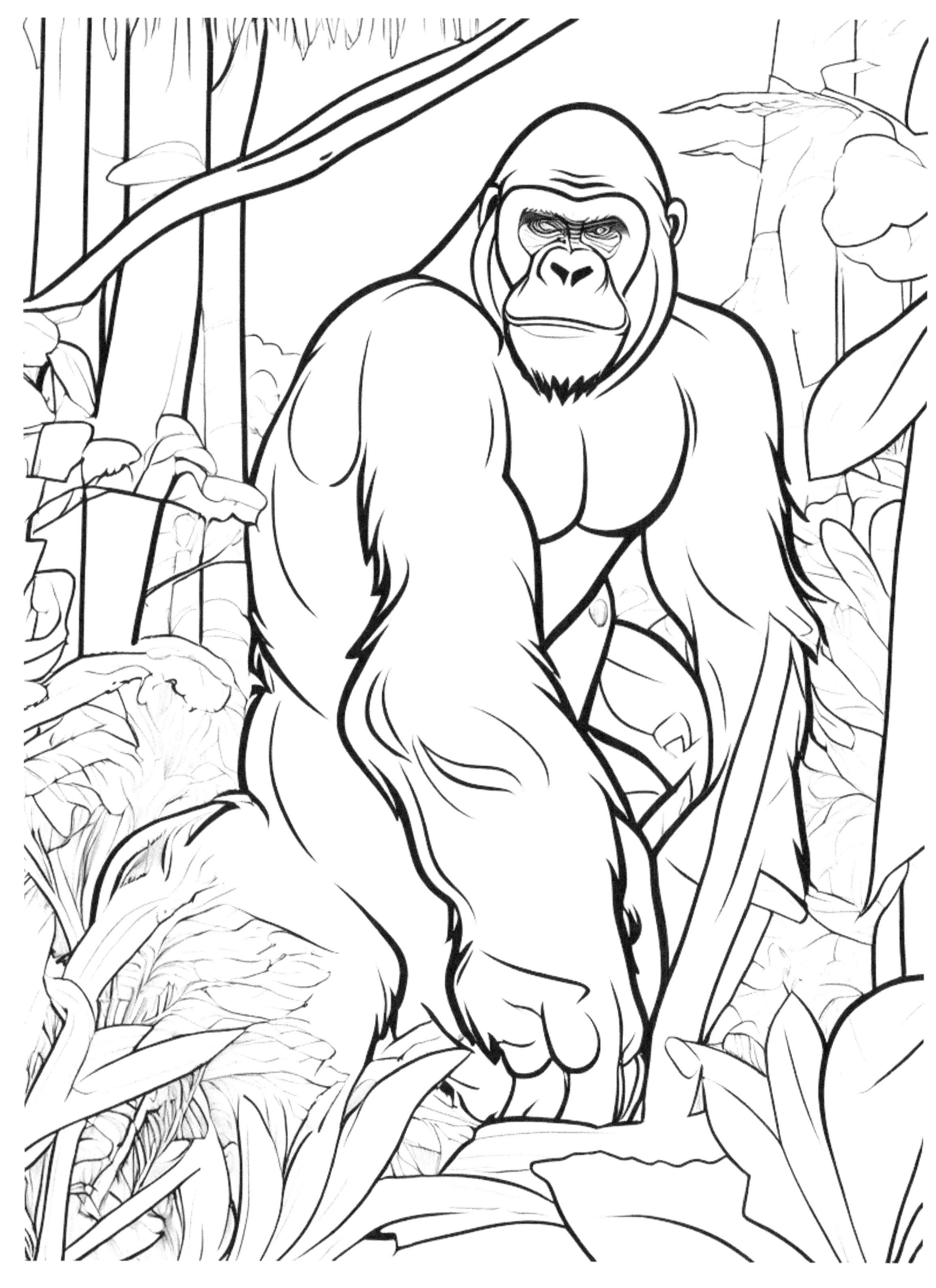

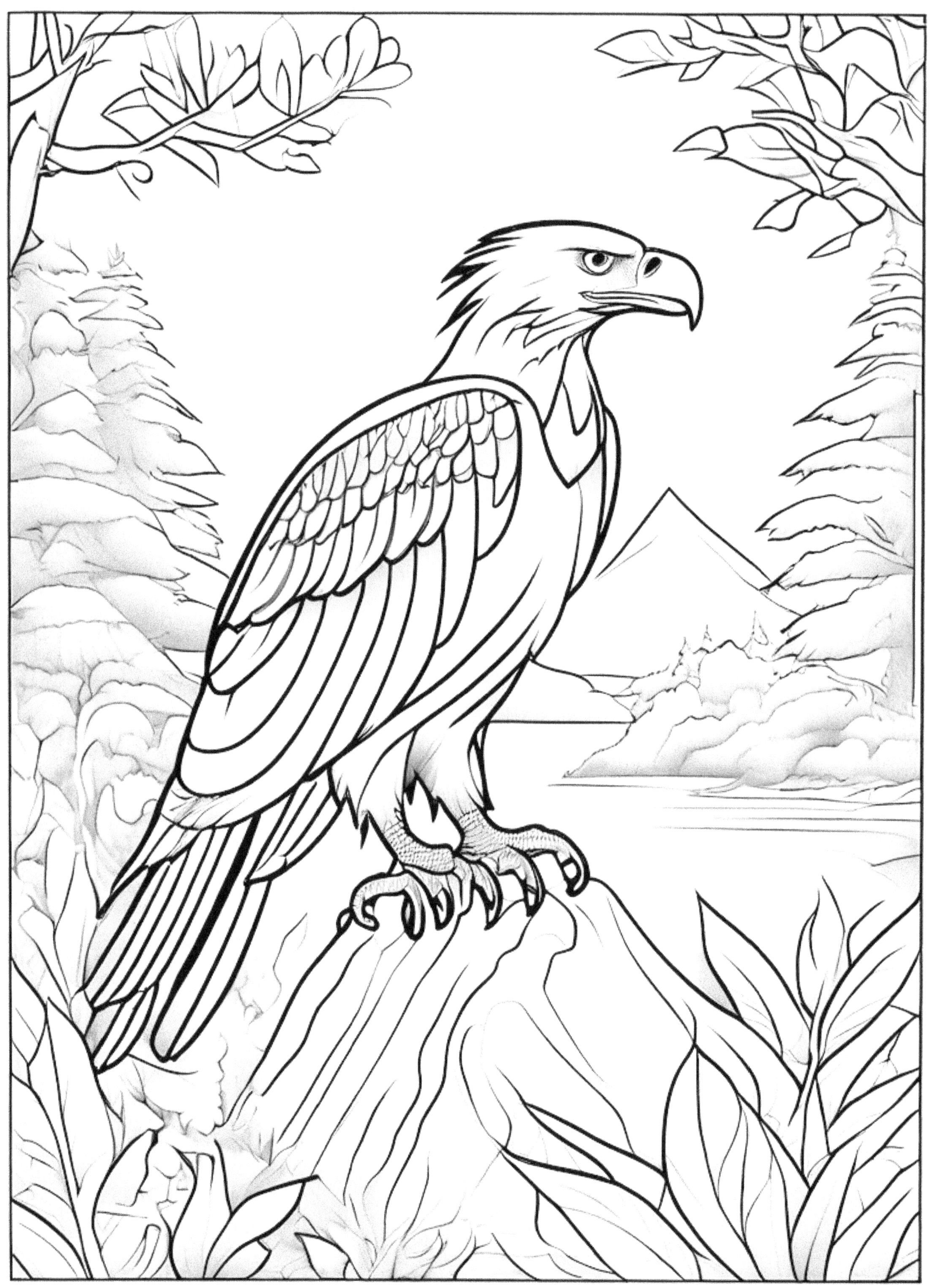